FROGS
of Australia

Marion Anstis

First published in 2017 by Reed New Holland Publishers
Sydney

Level 1, 178 Fox Valley Road, Wahroonga, NSW 2076, Australia

newhollandpublishers.com

A record of this book is held at the National Library of Australia.

ISBN 978 1 92151 790 7

Managing Director: Fiona Schultz
Publisher and Project Editor: Simon Papps
Designer: Andrew Davies
Production Director: Arlene Gippert
Printed in China

All text and images by Marion Anstis except for the following contributors
(images and accounts):

Hal Cogger (Southern Corroboree Frog, Southern Toadlet); Raelene Donelly (Spencer's Tree
Frog); Tim Hawkes (Wide-mouthed Frog, Mottled Barred Frog, Great Barred Frog, Eungella
Day Frog, Rain Whistling Frog, Buzzing Nursery Frog, Rattling Nursery Frog, Northern Ornate
Nursery Frog); Harry Hines (Kroombit Tops Tinker Frog); Greg Hollis (Baw Baw Frog); Michael
Mahony (Sandhill Frog, Northern Tinker Frog); David Nelson (Tasmanian Tree Frog, Moss
Froglet); Daniel O'Brien (Martin's Toadlet); Adam Parsons (Jervis Bay Tree Frog, Forest
Toadlet); Aaron Payne (Rough Frog, Large Toadlet); Evan Pickett (Green and Golden Bell Frog);
Narelle Power (Slender Tree Frog); Eric Vanderduys (Kutini Boulder Frog, Black Mountain
Boulder Frog).

10 9 8 7 6 5 4

Keep up with New Holland Publishers:
 NewHollandPublishers
 @newhollandpublishers

CONTENTS

Frog Families and genera

INTRODUCTION

Australia has a wide diversity of fascinating frogs which have adapted to a great diversity of habitats and climates across this large continent and its associated islands. Currently there are 249 species and subspecies described, but many others are expected to be named in the future as ongoing genetic studies uncover their true identity. Not all species can be covered in this book, but I have included a diverse range of the most commonly encountered, most interesting, rare, and more unusual frogs Australia has to offer.

The largest and most complex family is the **Hylidae** or Tree Frogs, most of which belong to the genus *Litoria*. This genus includes frogs which are very familiar to most people, such as the popular Green Tree Frog, which has become a household pet both here and internationally. Although the *Litoria* are often tree-dwellers and have suction discs on the ends of their fingers and toes to help them climb, a number of species live on the ground in forests or rocky areas such as streams and gorges, and a number of other predominantly ground-dwellers have only very small discs on their digits. Thirteen species from the family Hylidae belong to the related but very different group of burrowing frogs in the genus *Cyclorana*, which are known for their ability to remain underground for long periods, cocooned within their skin to protect them from dehydration. When they come to the surface after rain, they eat anything that moves and fits in their mouth, including metamorphosed frogs. They lack discs on their fingers and toes. All members of the family Hylidae have a horizontal pupil, all have aquatic tadpoles and all except *Litoria longirostris* lay their eggs in water.

INTRODUCTION

The Limnodynastid and Southern Frog families, **Limnodynastidae** and **Myobatrachidae**, are ground-dwellers and do not have discs on the tips of their fingers and toes because they don't normally climb much at all. They hide under logs, rocks or in the base of tussocks in moist areas, and a number of groups are burrowers. Adults range in size from very small species (15mm) to very large (up to about 120mm) and ground frogs are extremely varied in the ways they have adapted to living and breeding in Australia's diverse geography and unpredictable, often arid climate. While some genera have a horizontal pupil, a number have a vertical pupil (for example *Heleioporus*, *Mixophyes* and *Neobatrachus*). Many species of Limnodynastidae lay their eggs in floating foam masses, most in water, but some in burrows which later flood. All have aquatic tadpoles. The Myobatrachidae, however, have a great variety of breeding modes ranging from aquatic tadpoles to semi-terrestrial and terrestrial, and some are direct developers in which there is no true tadpole stage and the eggs develop into tiny froglets entirely within the egg capsule.

The Narrow-mouthed frogs, **Microhylidae**, are mostly small frogs (with one larger species which grows to just over 50mm) and all live in far north Queensland in rainforest, misty mountain tops and even in drier areas where huge outcrops of granite boulders provide ample hiding places. Many are great climbers and have expanded discs on their digits, but others secrete themselves under dense leaf litter, rocks or logs in damp forest. They are known for their direct development breeding mode in which the larger, unpigmented eggs are laid on land and the adult male protects them until the tiny froglets emerge from the eggs.

We have only one species which is classed as a 'True Frog', in the genus *Hylarana* belonging to the family **Ranidae**. They have aquatic tadpoles. The many other species of frogs from this family are otherwise found in the Americas, Europe and Asia.

The family **Bufonidae** (True Toads) has only one introduced representative in Australia, known as the Cane Toad, which after its introduction in 1935 into Queensland to control cane beetles, has unfortunately spread freely across the northern half of the continent. Its poison glands result in huge losses of most native animals which try to eat the toads and all stages of its life history are toxic. Female toads lay many thousands of eggs in water in long trailing chains. Native frogs by contrast lay far fewer eggs. Other than this non-native species, Australia has no native 'true' toads, although some are commonly called 'toadlets' because they look a bit like them.

Feeding

For the vast majority of the species covered in this book, individuals feed on small invertebrates, or on any moving creature than is smaller than the frog itself, often including other frogs. When a species has an interesting aspect to its diet – for example, the Magnificent Tree Frog which sometimes feeds on small bats – this has been noted in the 'Behaviour' section of the species account.

Breeding

Frogs all need at least moisture to survive and breed successfully, but it is not generally known that they don't all need water in which to lay their eggs. Unless otherwise stated in the text, the eggs are pigmented. In Australia, our frogs have six very different methods of breeding listed here in order from the most common method to the least common:

1. aquatic (eggs and tadpoles develop in water); 2. terrestrial/aquatic (eggs on land, tadpoles in water); 3. terrestrial (eggs and tadpoles develop in nest on land); 4. direct development (eggs on land – no tadpole stage, from egg to frog inside the egg capsule); 5. pouched brooding (newly hatched tiny tadpoles climb into pouches of adult male frog and later emerge as froglets); and 6. gastric brooding (eggs hatch and tadpoles develop inside stomach of adult female frog). Sadly our only two species of gastric brooders (genus *Rheobatrachus*) are now presumed extinct. When the breeding season begins, males call to females at night with their own individual call — some high-pitched, some low or in between, some with short notes, others long. As in birds, the female only responds to a male of her own species and moves nearer to the male, who then climbs on her back and grasps her (the process of amplexus). When she begins laying eggs, he fertilises them, and they are deposited in water or in a moist nest on land.

Tadpoles

All of our frogs, except for those with direct development, have a tadpole stage during which feeding and growth occurs, and limbs develop and increase in length towards metamorphosis. Aquatic tadpoles present a fascinating study for children and adults, and different species groups have very different adaptations to their habitat. Many stream-dwellers have a sucker mouth for hanging onto rocks in flowing water and a powerful tail for swimming against the current. Pond-dwellers don't need those features, but instead often develop bigger tail-fins and a fine tail-tip which are ideal for making sudden turns to rapidly escape predators and for cruising near the surface in still water. Aquatic tadpoles feed on algae, sediments on the bottom and other plant matter, but as they approach metamorphosis, they avidly devour any dead invertebrates or other protein in the water, which boosts their nutrition when they most need it to develop their limbs and change into frogs. Those which develop in a nest on land are very small and never need to feed through their mouth, as they have a large supply of yolk in their gut which sustains them right through until they become a tiny frog.

Metamorphosis

The remarkable transformation of a tadpole into a frog never ceases to invoke awe in those that watch it. Some Australian tadpole species can take up to two years from egg to reach metamorphosis if they live in cold water streams at higher altitude, while those in temporary ponds in hot climates can develop from egg to frog in as little as 11 days! But all have to go through enormous changes to become a frog, swapping gills for lungs, tadpole eyes for larger frog eyes, a spiral gut for a stomach and intestine (and other internal organs of the adult frog), a small tadpole mouth for a much wider frog mouth, and of course legs and arms and absorption of their tail. All this takes place rapidly, mostly over the last week or two of life as a tadpole, and a miniature version of the adult frog emerges from the water, land nest or the adult frog's brood pouches.

Threats

Frogs worldwide are dropping greatly in numbers as a result of disease, habitat loss, pollution and introduced predators. Nearly half of all known frog species are in decline globally and about 168 species are presumed extinct. While habitat destruction tops the list as the main reason for such drastic declines, the fungal skin disease known as 'Chytrid fungus' has devastated many frog species around the world. In Australia, we have lost five species presumably to this disease, with at least 49 others ranging from threatened to critically endangered. Some populations seem to have shown signs of recovery, but the combination of disease and environmental changes are likely to continue to put increasing pressure on their long-term survival prospects. The introduced Cane Toad has also had a strong impact on Australian native frogs because it is toxic throughout its life history, and as it invades new areas, native frogs that eat young toads, or native tadpoles that eat their eggs, will mostly die.

How can we help?

As the coastal habitats and forests favoured by so many frog species are consumed for housing and industry, and inland habitats including our precious water table are greatly impacted and often destroyed by mining and land clearing, it is likely that many Australian frogs across most habitats face a very uncertain existence in the next 20–50 years and beyond. More recently some suitable replacement breeding habitats have been created, such as when new highways are constructed, which is good to see. We can all help by avoiding use of pesticides near water, never releasing aquarium fish in waterways, and never transporting and releasing frogs or tadpoles to a different site (which can spread disease). We can create or regenerate suitable habitats in bushland, farmland or even suburban gardens, and raise awareness through social media of the need for a reasonable balance to be struck between habitat alteration and the needs of frogs for unpolluted natural places in which to live and breed. In return we will benefit because frogs are good indicators of a polluted environment, especially in relation to our most valuable resource, water.

The species in this book

In this book I have tried to include a broad coverage of 180 of the 249 Australian frog species from all families. Many are widespread in distribution and more well-known to people, while others are included because they are endangered or of special interest due to their unusual features or breeding biology. Each species account contains information which is important for identification, including size, colour, behaviour, habitat, range and call. While coverage cannot be comprehensive in a volume of this size, it is hoped that the book will encourage newcomers to the subject and provide a quick initial reference for use in the field, being a very handy size for a pocket or backpack. Above all I hope that it will inspire and encourage interest in the study and conservation of our remarkable and mostly endemic Australian frogs, so that we can all help protect them for future generations. For a fully comprehensive guide to frogs and tadpoles, see *Tadpoles and Frogs of Australia* by Marion Anstis and other books in the Additional Reading section.

GLOSSARY

Amplexus: Pairing of adult male and female frog prior to egg-laying
Breeding mode: Particular way of laying eggs in water or on land
Digit: Finger or toe
Direct development: When fertilised eggs develop to frog inside jelly capsule without a tadpole stage
Granular: Rough, e.g. skin
Invertebrates: Animals without a backbone, e.g. insects, spiders
Lyrate: Lyre-shaped marking
Metatarsal tubercle: Firm nodule on edge of foot
Parotoid gland: Swollen sac containing secretions on shoulder
Semi-terrestrial: Partly on land and in water
Terrestrial: On land
Tubercle: Small protuberance or nodule
Tympanum: Ear
Vertebral: Backbone region

FURTHER READING

Anstis, M. 2013. *Tadpoles and Frogs of Australia*. Reed New Holland.

Anstis, M. 2002. *Tadpoles of South-eastern Australia*. Reed New Holland.

Cogger, H.G. 2014. *Reptiles and Amphibians of Australia*. CSIRO Publishing.

Hoskin, C., and Hero, J-M. 2008. *Rainforest Frogs of the Wet Tropics*. Griffith University.

Tyler, M.J., and Doughty, P. 2009. *Field Guide to Frogs of Western Australia*. Western Australian Museum.

Vanderduys, E. 2012. *Field Guide to the Frogs of Queensland*. CSIRO Publishing.

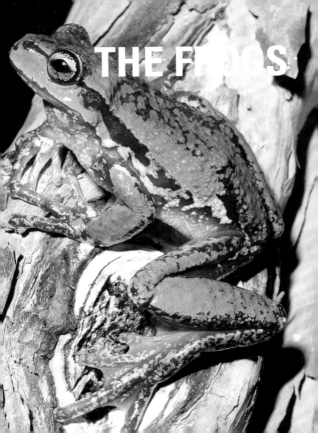

THE FROGS

STRIPED BURROWING FROG
Cyclorana alboguttata

SIZE/ID: ♂ to 67mm, ♀ to 83mm. Brown or grey-brown, many with darker patches and pale vertebral stripe. May have olive-green on side of head. Skin with tubercles and often elongate folds. Toes 1/2 webbed.

HABITAT/RANGE: Very common across north-east Qld and NSW. Woodland, plains and drier forest, usually in clay soil.

BEHAVIOUR: Burrower. Surfaces after first heavy rain in spring/summer. Egg clumps in ponds, billabongs and ditches. ♂ calls on ground near water.

CALL: Loud, repeated 'quacking', often in deafening choruses.

GIANT BURROWING FROG *Cyclorana australis*

SIZE/ID: ♂ to 85mm, ♀ to 105mm. Green, brown or grey, with or without darker patches and a pale vertebral stripe. Dark stripe on side. Skin has fine, low tubercles and longitudinal fold. Toes 1/3 webbed.

HABITAT/RANGE: Very common across northern Australia from WA to western Qld in woodland and open grassland.

BEHAVIOUR: Burrower. Surfaces after first heavy rain in spring/summer. Egg clumps in ponds, billabongs and ditches. ♂ calls on ground near water.

CALL: Long sequence of loud 'honks'.

SHORT-FOOTED FROG *Cyclorana brevipes*

SIZE/ID: ♂ and ♀ to 45mm. Shades of brown to yellow-brown marbled with pale or dark patches. Cream vertebral stripe, pale collar behind eyes. Skin smooth to slightly granular. Toes webbed at base.

HABITAT/RANGE: Common from north NSW through Qld and just into NT. Savannah woodland on clay soil.

BEHAVIOUR: Burrower, surfaces after first heavy rain in spring to autumn. Egg clumps in flooded ditches or ponds. ♂ calls on ground beside water.

CALL: Long, drawn-out low-pitched wail or growl.

HIDDEN-EAR FROG *Cyclorana cryptotis*

SIZE/ID: ♂ to 44mm, ♀ to 46mm. Brown to rusty red, grey or greenish, usually with diffuse darker or paler markings and paler vertebral stripe. Tympanum hidden. Skin has numerous fine tubercles. Toes to about 1/2 webbed.

HABITAT/RANGE: Common across northern Australia from WA to north-west Qld. Savannah woodland on clay or lateritic soil.

BEHAVIOUR: Burrower, surfaces after heavy rain in spring to autumn. Egg clumps in flooded grassland, ditches or ponds. ♂ calls while afloat, or from base of tussock beside pond.

CALL: Low-pitched moan or growl rising at end.

LONG-FOOTED FROG *Cyclorana longipes*

SIZE/ID: ♂ to 46mm, ♀ to 55mm. Pale grey below, yellow-brown above with dark brown patches. Cream vertebral stripe and often a pale collar behind eyes. Skin may have slightly raised longitudinal folds and some low tubercles. Toes 1/3 webbed.

HABITAT/RANGE: Common across northern Australia from WA to NT. Savannah woodland on clay or sandy soils.

BEHAVIOUR: Burrower, surfaces after first heavy rain in spring/ summer. Egg clumps in flooded ditch or pond. ♂ calls while afloat, or from base of tussock.

CALL: Low-pitched, slightly quavering nasal growl ending with slight upward inflection.

MAIN'S FROG *Cylorana maini*

SIZE/ID: ♂ to 46mm, ♀ to 47mm. Dull brown to beige with small darker patches; often a cream vertebral stripe and paler collar behind eyes. Skin has fine low tubercles. Toes 1/3 webbed.

HABITAT/RANGE: Very common across arid central Australia from WA to NT. Sandy to clay soil.

BEHAVIOUR: Burrower, surfaces after heavy rain. Eggs laid in clumps in waterhole, river or billabong in spring/summer wet season. ♂ calls while afloat, or from base of tussock beside pond.

CALL: Fairly high-pitched wail with a distinct tremor likened to bleating sheep.

WESTERN WATER-HOLDING FROG
Cyclorana occidentalis

SIZE/ID: ♂ to 58mm, ♀ to at least 66mm. Broad body with prominent golden eyes tilted upwards. Yellow-brown to reddish-brown, some with darker patches. Skin has tubercles and longitudinal skin folds. Toes fully webbed.

HABITAT/RANGE: Arid to semi-arid areas in central WA. Often in river floodplains with clay soil.

BEHAVIOUR: Burrower, surfaces after heavy summer rain. Eggs laid in clumps in claypan, pond or overflow from river after flooding. ♂ calls while afloat in water.

CALL: Drawn-out, low-pitched, nasal 'waaaaaarrrh' with upward inflection at end.

WIDE-MOUTHED FROG *Cyclorana novaehollandiae*

SIZE/ID: ♂ to 81mm, ♀ to 101mm. Big broad head, very wide mouth, projecting snout, mottled upper lip. Shades of brown to yellow-brown sometimes with a pale vertebral stripe, dark bar from below eye to upper lip. Skin has longitudinal folds and low tubercles. Toes 1/3 webbed.

HABITAT/RANGE: Qld and just into north-west NSW. Woodland or grassland on clay or sandy soils.

BEHAVIOUR: Burrower, surfaces after first heavy spring/summer rains. Egg clumps in flooded plains, grasslands, ditches or ponds. ♂ calls on ground near water.

CALL: Loud, explosive 'unk', repeated continuously.

WATER-HOLDING FROG *Cylorana platycephala*

SIZE/ID: ♂ to 64mm, ♀ to at least 72mm. Broad body, eyes tilted upwards. Grey or brown with or without green or pink tinges. Skin smooth, sometimes with fine tubercles. Toes fully webbed.

HABITAT/RANGE: Inland NSW, Qld and eastern NT. Woodland to more arid plains in clay soil.

BEHAVIOUR: Burrower, surfaces after heavy spring/summer rain, mostly aquatic when active. Egg clumps in flooded pools. ♂ calls from shallow water.

CALL: Low-pitched, drawn-out growl with upward inflection at end.

ROUGH FROG *Cylorana verrucosa*

SIZE/ID: ♂ to 45mm, ♀ to 49mm. Short, stocky body. Light brown with green patches, or all green. Skin with tubercles and folds. Toes 1/3 webbed.

HABITAT/RANGE: Inland northern NSW, southern Qld. Woodland, floodplains and rural land, often in clay soil. Often confused with similar unnamed species from north-west NSW and Qld which is never as green.

BEHAVIOUR: Burrower, surfaces after heavy spring/summer rain. Eggs laid in clumps in pools. ♂ calls from ground near water.

CALL: Low-pitched, quavering moan with slight upward inflection at end.

SLENDER TREE FROG *Litoria adelaidensis*

SIZE/ID: ♂ to 45mm, ♀ to 60mm. Elongate, slender frog, brown and/or green with broad dark brown stripe along sides, white stripe below. Sides may be dappled with white spots. Skin smooth. Digits with discs, toes 3/4 webbed.

HABITAT/RANGE: Only in south-west Australia; inhabits forest, swamps, farmlands and gardens.

BEHAVIOUR: Tree-dweller. Eggs laid in clusters attached to vegetation in permanent ponds and swamps after spring/summer rain. ♂ calls day and night from well above water, on ground or in water.

CALL: Loud, low, harsh 'grating screech'.

GREEN AND GOLDEN BELL FROG *Litoria aurea*

SIZE/ID: ♂ to 69mm, ♀ to 108mm. Green with gold stripe on side, often gold marks on back, turquoise in groin and undersurfaces of thighs. Skin smooth, smooth tubercles over sides. Digits with small discs, toes 3/4 webbed.

HABITAT/RANGE: Endangered, once common along east coast of NSW and Vic. Inhabits coastal forest, farmland and some islands.

BEHAVIOUR: Ground-dweller. Eggs laid in lagoons, swamps and permanent ponds after spring/summer rain. ♂ calls while afloat among vegetation.

CALL: Low-pitched, quavering growl with downward inflection at end.

BARRINGTON TOPS TREE FROG
Litoria barringtonensis

SIZE/ID: ♂ to 29mm, ♀ to 37mm. Bright green when active, with scattered small black spots; dull bronze-brown when inactive. Thin gold stripe from snout to arm. Skin smooth. Digits with discs, toes 3/4 webbed.

HABITAT/RANGE: Forest in ranges of mid- to north-east NSW.

BEHAVIOUR: Stream-dweller. Eggs laid in clumps in shallow rock pool after spring/summer rain. ♂ calls on vegetation beside stream pool.

CALL: Three notes: drawn out 'we-e-eet' followed by lower, soft 'toc, toc'.

NORTHERN SEDGE FROG *Litoria bicolor*

SIZE/ID: ♂ to 27mm, ♀ to 29mm. Bronze or green, often with broad golden-brown band down back. Bronze stripe along side and head, white stripe below. Skin smooth. Digits with discs, toes 3/4 webbed.

HABITAT/RANGE: Common throughout north Qld. Open forest and paperbark swamps.

BEHAVIOUR: Tree-dweller. Eggs laid in small clusters in ditches, lagoons and ponds after rain in summer/autumn. ♂ calls from emergent reeds or shrubs.

CALL: Rapid, rasp or rolling sound often with some short pips.

BOOROOLONG FROG *Litoria booroolongensis*

SIZE/ID: ♂ to 42mm, ♀ to 54mm. Lean, muscular build. Grey-brown, olive-brown or reddish-brown with diffuse mottling. Skin with fine tubercles. Distinct discs on digits, toes almost fully webbed.

HABITAT/RANGE: Endangered. Rocky streams of NSW from New England Ranges to near Cooma.

BEHAVIOUR: Stream-dweller. Strong jumper and climber. Eggs laid in clump on or under rock in shallow stream pool after spring/summer rain. ♂ calls from rock near water.

CALL: Soft 'purr', difficult to hear above sound of water.

GREEN-THIGHED FROG *Litoria brevipalmata*

SIZE/ID: ♂ to 43mm, ♀ to 47mm. Chocolate brown with green mottling on groin and thighs. Dark stripe on side of head and body, white stripe on upper lip. Skin smooth. Small discs on digits, toes webbed at base.

HABITAT/RANGE: Vulnerable. North of Sydney, NSW, to south-east Qld. Coastal forests and swamps.

BEHAVIOUR: Ground-dweller. Eggs laid in floating film in ephemeral pond after heavy rain in late spring/summer. ♂ calls from log or ground near water.

CALL: Long series of rapid 'quacks' lasting up to two minutes, increasing in rate and volume.

TASMANIAN TREE FROG *Litoria burrowsae*

SIZE/ID: ♂ to 53mm, ♀ to 60mm. Green to dark brown with scattered brown or gold flecks or patches. Sides, inner thighs, hands and feet mottled brown and white. Dark stripe on side. Skin smooth or granular. Digits with discs, toes 3/4 webbed.

HABITAT/RANGE: Endemic to Tasmania; forest, moorland and alpine habitats. In decline.

BEHAVIOUR: Tree-dweller. Egg clusters attached to vegetation in pool after winter to summer rain. ♂ calls from tree or vegetation in or beside water.

CALL: Series of 'goose-like' honks.

GREEN TREE FROG *Litoria caerulea*

SIZE/ID: ♂ to 77mm, ♀ to 110mm. Green, sometimes with white spots. May have yellow hands and feet. Inland NSW populations smaller and often blue-green. Skin smooth. Digits with broad discs, toes 3/4 webbed.

HABITAT/RANGE: Widespread across northern half of Australia in woodland, forest, coastal areas and smaller towns; declined in cities.

BEHAVIOUR: Tree-dweller. Eggs laid in floating clusters in ephemeral ponds after heavy summer storms. ♂ calls from tree, downpipe or ground near water.

CALL: Series of loud, low-pitched 'crawk, crawk' notes.

RED-EYED TREE FROG *Litoria chloris*

SIZE/ID: ♂ to 62mm, ♀ to 68mm. Green with large orange-red eyes. Sides and belly yellow, backs of thighs purple. Skin smooth. Broad discs on digits, fingers 3/4 webbed, toes fully webbed.

HABITAT/RANGE: East coast and lower ranges from north of Sydney, NSW, to Mackay, Qld. Forest and farmland, declining in some areas.

BEHAVIOUR: Tree-dweller. Egg clusters in ephemeral pools or creeks after heavy summer storms. ♂ calls from low vegetation or ground near water.

CALL: Series of wailing notes with upward inflection, short higher-pitched chirps at end.

BLUE MOUNTAINS TREE FROG *Litoria citropa*

SIZE/ID: ♂ to 57mm, ♀ to 65mm. Golden-brown, green along side of head, body and on limbs, brown flecks. Armpits, groin and underparts of legs red. Skin smooth to finely granular. Broad discs on digits, toes 1/2 webbed.

HABITAT/RANGE: South-east coast and ranges from south of Newcastle, NSW, to north-east Vic. Rocky sandstone streams in forest and heathland.

BEHAVIOUR: Eggs scattered on bottom of rock pool after spring/ summer rain. ♂ calls from rock or vegetation.

CALL: Soft, longer low-pitched note followed by a few short quick croaks run together.

COOLOOLA SEDGE FROG *Litoria cooloolensis*

SIZE/ID: ♂ to 26mm, ♀ to 30mm. Green or golden-brown, may be peppered with minute black dots. White stripe on side of head to upper arm. Skin finely granular. Distinct discs on digits, toes up to almost fully webbed.

HABITAT/RANGE: Endangered. Coastal south-east Qld, Stradbroke and Fraser Islands. Restricted to sandy lakes and lagoons.

BEHAVIOUR: Tree-dweller. Egg clusters attached to reeds after spring to autumn rain. ♂ calls from tall reed above water.

CALL: Rising 'wre-e-et' followed by a rolling lower-pitched rattle.

COPLAND'S ROCK FROG *Litoria coplandi*

SIZE/ID: ♂ to 36mm, ♀ to 43mm. Brown to reddish-brown, often with indistinct darker mottling. Head broad, body and limbs muscular. Skin finely granular. Broad discs on digits, toes almost fully webbed.

HABITAT/RANGE: Across northern WA and NT, especially in escarpments. Rocky rivers, streams or creeks.

BEHAVIOUR: Ground-dweller among rocks. Strong jumper. Egg clusters attached to rocks in pools after spring/summer rain. ♂ calls from rock near water.

CALL: A series of high-pitched, short, quavering notes.

35

SPOTTED-THIGHED FROG *Litoria cyclorhyncha*

SIZE/ID: ♂ to 66mm, ♀ to 77mm. Grey to golden with green patches. Side of belly, armpit and inner leg black with whitish spots. Skin smooth with scattered tubercles. Digits with small discs, toes almost fully webbed.

HABITAT/RANGE: Coastal to partly inland south-west WA east of Albany to Hopetoun. Woodland, forest, partly cleared land in permanent ponds.

BEHAVIOUR: Ground-dweller. Egg clusters in ponds or dams after heavy spring/summer rain. ♂ calls while afloat among vegetation.

CALL: Low-pitched growl similar to sawing wood.

DAHL'S AQUATIC FROG *Litoria dahlii*

SIZE/ID: ♂ to 63mm, ♀ to 71mm. Green and golden, often with pale green vertebral stripe and variable gold or dark patches. Skin finely granular. No discs on claw-like fingers, very small discs on fully-webbed toes.

HABITAT/RANGE: Northern Australia (Northern Territory). Separate populations in north-west Qld. Lakes and billabongs.

BEHAVIOUR: Aquatic; feeds in water on invertebrates, frogs and tadpoles. Eggs laid in water after rain during summer wet season. ♂ calls while afloat among vegetation.

CALL: Long, low-pitched 'wa-a-a-a-r' lasting 2–3 seconds and repeated at short intervals.

AUSTRALIAN LACE-LID *Litoria dayi*

SIZE/ID: ♂ to 42mm, ♀ to 60mm. Immaculate brown or reddish-brown with or without diffuse darker mottling and irregular white spots. Large dark brown eyes with lacy-white lower eyelid. Skin smooth to finely granular. Large discs on digits, fingers partly webbed, toes fully webbed.

HABITAT/RANGE: Fast-flowing rocky streams in Wet Tropics, north Qld.

BEHAVIOUR: Stream-dweller. Clump of white eggs beneath rock in stream pools or riffles at any time. ♂ calls from rock or shrub near water.

CALL: Soft, quavering 'creeee' sometimes with mixed shorter notes.

Note unique eyelids.

BLEATING TREE FROG *Litoria dentata*

SIZE/ID: ♂ to 40mm, ♀ to 44mm. Pale to dark brown above with a broad darker brown band down back. Snout bluntly rounded, eye dark copper-red. Skin smooth. Broad discs on digits, fingers 1/3 webbed, toes 3/4 webbed.

HABITAT/RANGE: East coast and ranges of NSW and south Qld. Woodland, forest and farmland.

BEHAVIOUR: Tree-dweller. Eggs spread over substrate in ephemeral ponds after heavy summer rain. ♂ calls from tree then ground near water.

CALL: Continuous, long, shrill, high-pitched quavering trill or bleating.

BROWN TREE FROG *Litoria ewingii*

SIZE/ID: ♂ to 40mm, ♀ to 46mm. Light to dark brown or red-brown with broad darker brown band down back, divided in some. Dark stripe along side of head. Skin with fine tubercles. Distinct discs on digits, fingers 1/3 webbed, toes 3/4 webbed.

HABITAT/RANGE: South-east coast and ranges of NSW, Vic, south-east SA and Tas. Forest, farmland, heath, alpine and suburban areas.

BEHAVIOUR: Tree-dweller. Small, fluid egg clusters attached to vegetation in ponds after rain. ♂ calls from vegetation near water.

CALL: Series of whirring 'reet, reet, reet' notes.

EASTERN DWARF SEDGE FROG *Litoria fallax*

SIZE/ID: ♂ to 26mm, ♀ to 32mm. Green or bronze and green, dark stripe on side and white stripe below eye to arm. Skin smooth. Distinct discs on digits, fingers webbed at base, toes 3/4 webbed.

HABITAT/RANGE: East coast and ranges from Qld to Vic. Permanent ponds with emergent reeds in forest, farmland and coastal wallum swamps.

BEHAVIOUR: Tree-dweller. Small egg clusters attached to vegetation mainly after spring/summer rain. ♂ calls from reed or grass above water.

CALL: Penetrating 'wre-e-e-k' with upward inflection.

WALLUM ROCKET FROG *Litoria freycineti*

SIZE/ID: ♂ to 39mm, ♀ to 42mm. Light to darker brown with large dark patches, broad dark stripe on side, white stripe beneath eye to arm. Skin with small tubercles. Small discs on digits, toes about 1/2 webbed.

HABITAT/RANGE: East coast from south-east Qld to south of Sydney, NSW. Forest, heathland and coastal wallum swamps, creeks and ponds.

BEHAVIOUR: Ground-dweller, strong jumper. Eggs scattered over substrate in pools after spring/summer rain. ♂ calls on ground near water.

CALL: Long sequence of loud 'chuck' notes.

DAINTY TREE FROG *Litoria gracilenta*

SIZE/ID: ♂ to 42mm, ♀ to
45mm. Green. Underparts
and limbs yellow. Dark red
and purple tops of thighs.
Fingers 3/4 webbed, toes
fully webbed.

HABITAT/RANGE: Forest,
farmland and swamps from
Cape York to Sydney.

BEHAVIOUR: Tree-dweller. Floating egg clusters in ephemeral ponds.

CALL: Long, low, growl.

BUMPY ROCKET FROG *Litoria inermis*

SIZE/ID: ♂ to 33mm, ♀ to
37mm. Brown with diffuse
darker markings, black and
white bars on lower lip.
Very small discs on digits.

HABITAT/RANGE: North
Australia from south-east
Qld to Kimberley, WA.
Grassy floodplains and forest.

BEHAVIOUR: Ground-dweller. Eggs laid in clusters in ponds.

CALL: Complex series of 'chuck-chuck' and short trills.

WHITE-LIPPED TREE FROG *Litoria infrafrenata*

SIZE/ID: ♂ to 102mm, ♀ to 135mm. Our largest tree frog. Bright to dark green or brown, rarely yellow, with white lower lip. Skin smooth above, broad smooth tubercles over sides. Large discs on digits, fingers 1/2 webbed, toes fully webbed.

HABITAT/RANGE: North Qld Wet Tropics to Cape York. Forests, swamps, suburban gardens and plantations.

BEHAVIOUR: Invertebrates and small mammals. Tree-dweller. Egg clusters in pools during spring/summer wet season. ♂ calls from trees and shrubs near water.

CALL: Loud, low-pitched rapid two-note 'da-dak' repeated regularly.

JERVIS BAY TREE FROG *Litoria jervisiensis*

SIZE/ID: ♂ to 37mm, ♀ to 44mm. Brown with broad darker brown divided patch down back, pale streak under eye. Back of thighs red; armpits, groin and front of legs yellow. Skin smooth. Distinct discs on digits, toes fully webbed.

HABITAT/RANGE: Coast and eastern lower ranges NSW to north-east Vic in forest, heath and swamps.

BEHAVIOUR: Tree-dweller. Egg clusters attached to reeds in ponds, lagoons and swamps after rain in autumn to spring. ♂ calls from reed or branch over pond.

CALL: Short series of low-pitched whirring 'reeet-reeet' notes.

BROAD-PALMED FROG *Litoria latopalmata*

SIZE/ID: ♂ to 39mm, ♀ to 42mm. Brown, often with dark flecks. Broad paler band down middle of head and body. Dark stripe on side of head, white bars on lip. Groin and back of thigh yellow and black. Skin mostly smooth. Small discs on digits, toes almost fully webbed.

HABITAT/RANGE: Eastern half of Qld, NSW, just into NT. Forests, coastal swamps, woodland, plains.

BEHAVIOUR: Ground-dweller, strong jumper. Floating egg clumps in pond after spring/summer rain. ♂ calls on ground near water.

CALL: Long series of rapid 'yap-yap' notes increasing in speed and volume.

HEATH FROG *Litoria littlejohni*

SIZE/ID: ♂ to 51mm, ♀ to 68mm. Grey-brown to yellow-brown with darker mottling or flecks, indistinct broad, divided darker band down back. Dark stripe on sides of head, inner legs, groin and armpits red. Skin smooth. Broad discs on digits, toes almost fully webbed.

HABITAT/RANGE: South-eastern NSW to north-east Vic in forests, woodland and heathland.

BEHAVIOUR: Tree-dweller. Egg clusters attached to vegetation in ponds and creeks after winter/spring rain. ♂ calls from shrubs or trees near water.

CALL: Series of drawn-out 'reet, reet, reet' notes.

LONG-SNOUTED TREE FROG *Litoria longirostris*

SIZE/ID: ♂ and ♀ to 27mm. Yellow-brown to pale brown, some with dark or pale patches. White streak beneath eye to arm. Skin with small tubercles. Discs on digits, toes to 3/4 webbed.

HABITAT/RANGE: Three ranges in Cape York Peninsula, Qld. Small creeks in rainforests.

BEHAVIOUR: Tree-dweller. Green eggs laid in cluster on leaf or trunk above pool. Only Australian tree frog to lay eggs out of water. Hatched tadpoles drop into water below. ♂ calls from perch above creek.

CALL: Short 'chirp' with or without soft rattles.

ARMOURED MIST FROG *Litoria lorica*

SIZE/ID: ♂ to 32mm, ♀ to 41mm. Shades of beige, brown or golden-brown with darker mottling. Eyes large, reticulated with gold. Skin finely granular. Large white discs on digits, fingers webbed at base, toes fully webbed.

HABITAT/RANGE: Critically endangered, known only from one locality in north Queensland. Fast-flowing rocky streams and rivers.

BEHAVIOUR: Stream-dweller. Sits on wet rocks or vertical rock faces in splash zone of small waterfalls. Breeds in flowing streams, possibly at any time of year.

CALL: Unknown.

ROCKHOLE FROG *Litoria meiriana*

SIZE/ID: ♂ to 20mm, ♀ to 22mm. Second smallest Australian hylid frog. Mottled brown or reddish-brown on lighter background, white and brown bars on lips. Skin with scattered tubercles, white-tipped on sides of body. Distinct discs on digits, toes almost fully webbed.

HABITAT/RANGE: Northern Australia, NT to WA. Rocky creeks and gorges.

BEHAVIOUR: Stream-dweller. Capable of skimming across surface of water. Egg clusters attached to rock in small pool during spring/summer wet season. ♂ calls from rock face or crevice beside pool.

CALL: Short 'repeated 'chick…chick' notes with occasional trill-like note.

JAVELIN FROG *Litoria microbelos*

SIZE/ID: ♂ to 16mm, ♀ to 18mm. Smallest Australian hylid frog. Brown with light brown band down back, dark stripe along sides, white below. Skin mostly smooth. Small discs on digits, toes about 1/3 webbed.

HABITAT/RANGE: Northern Australia, WA, NT to Arnhem Land and separate populations in north Qld. *Melaleuca* swamps, ponds, billabongs and flooded grassland.

BEHAVIOUR: Tree-dweller. Egg clusters attached to vegetation during spring/summer wet season. ♂ calls from grass, leaf or branch above water.

CALL: Series of high-pitched buzzing notes like a small cicada.

MOTORBIKE FROG *Litoria moorei*

SIZE/ID: ♂ to 71mm, ♀ to 78mm. Green to dark olive, variable gold and brown stripes and spots, often a pale vertebral stripe. Groin and undersides of legs blue-green. Skin with scattered tubercles. Small discs on digits, toes almost fully webbed.

HABITAT/RANGE: South-west WA, west coast to ranges, Rottnest Island. Swamps, lakes, ponds, rivers in forest and coastal areas.

BEHAVIOUR: Ground-dweller. Egg clusters in ponds after late winter to summer rain. ♂ calls while afloat.

CALL: Long, low-pitched growl like a motorcycle changing gears.

WATERFALL FROG *Litoria nannotis*

SIZE/ID: ♂ to 52mm, ♀ to 65mm. Shades of cream, brown or green with darker mottling all over. Eyes large, reticulated with gold. Skin finely granular. Large pale discs on digits, fingers webbed at base, toes 3/4 to fully webbed.

HABITAT/RANGE: Qld Wet Tropics. Fast-flowing rocky streams in rainforest and drier forest.

BEHAVIOUR: Stream-dweller. White eggs laid in clump under rock in stream. ♂ calls from rock in splash zone of small waterfalls.

CALL: Series of soft 'clucks', each with slight inflection at end.

ROCKET FROG *Litoria nasuta*

SIZE/ID: ♂ to 45mm, ♀ to 56mm. Light to darker brown or yellow, dark stripes down back and sides, some with broad paler band down back or darker patches. Skin with scattered tubercles and folds. Small discs on digits, toes about 1/2 webbed.

HABITAT/RANGE: Mid-north coastal NSW to Cape York, northern NT and WA. Swamps, open forest, grassy floodplains.

BEHAVIOUR: Ground-dweller, strong jumper. Floating egg clusters in pools after spring/summer rain. ♂ calls from ground near water.

CALL: Complex series of short 'chucks' with very short notes at end.

TAWNY ROCKET FROG *Litoria nigrofrenata*

SIZE/ID: ♂ to 42mm, ♀ to 46mm. Grey or red-brown, dark stripe on side of head to beyond arm, pale to yellow flush over side. Skin smooth. Small discs on digits, toes 3/4 webbed.

HABITAT/RANGE: North Qld, Wet Tropics to Cape York. Forest, woodland, creeks, swamps.

BEHAVIOUR: Ground-dweller, strong jumper. Egg clumps in ephemeral pools in spring/summer wet season. ♂ calls on ground near water.

CALL: Repeated nasal 'neep, neep', may end with series of lower 'chucks'.

WALLUM SEDGE FROG *Litoria olongburensis*

SIZE/ID: ♂ to 29mm, ♀ to 34mm. Endangered. Green or bronze, dark stripe on sides of head to past arm, white stripe below. Skin smooth with smooth tubercles along sides. Distinct discs on digits, toes 2/3 webbed.

HABITAT/RANGE: Coastal Qld and islands to north-east NSW. Wallum swamps and lakes.

BEHAVIOUR: Tree-dweller. Small egg clusters attached to reeds after spring/summer rain. ♂ calls from reed above water.

CALL: Rolling rasp with slight upward inflection at end.

VICTORIAN TREE FROG *Litoria paraewingi*

SIZE/ID: ♂ to 33mm, ♀ to 36mm. Light to dark brown with broad faintly divided darker brown band down back. Dark stripe along side of head. Skin smooth. Distinct discs on digits, toes almost fully webbed.

HABITAT/RANGE: Restricted to plains of central to northern Vic. Woodland, parks, grassland.

BEHAVIOUR: Tree-dweller. Fluid egg clusters attached to vegetation in ponds or creek pools after winter/spring rain. ♂ calls while afloat or from branch above water.

CALL: Series of 'wreet, wreet' notes rising in pitch towards end.

PEARSON'S STREAM FROG *Litoria pearsoniana*

SIZE/ID: ♂ to 29mm, ♀ to 37mm. Green to shades of brown, some with scattered dark dots. Dark stripe on side of head to arm, thin gold line above. Skin smooth. Broad discs on digits, toes almost fully webbed.

HABITAT/RANGE: Ranges of south-east Qld and northern NSW. Streams in forest.

BEHAVIOUR: Stream-dweller. Egg clusters attached to substrate of stream pool after spring/summer rain. ♂ calls from rock or vegetation near pool.

CALL: Soft, high-pitched 'we-ee-ek' with upward inflection followed by a few lower 'toc' notes.

PERON'S TREE FROG *Litoria peronii*

SIZE/ID: ♂ to 53mm, ♀ to 70mm. Brown to pale grey with green flecks and often darker patches. Yellow and black mottling in armpit, groin and inner thigh. Skin with fine tubercles. Large discs on digits, fingers 1/2 webbed, toes almost fully webbed.

HABITAT/RANGE: South-east Qld, NSW, Vic and eastern SA. Forest, woodland, coastal heath, swamps, urban areas.

BEHAVIOUR: Tree-dweller. Eggs laid singly and in small groups on vegetation in permanent ponds after spring/summer rain. ♂ calls on branch or ground near water.

CALL: Loud, rolling 'brrrrrrr...' with downward inflection at end.

GREEN STREAM FROG *Litoria phyllochroa*

SIZE/ID: ♂ to 32mm, ♀ to 40mm. Green to dark green, thin gold stripe on side of head to arm often with brown line beneath. Armpit, groin and inner thigh yellow. Skin smooth. Broad discs on digits, fingers 1/2 webbed, toes almost fully webbed.

HABITAT/RANGE: Coast and ranges NSW, Sydney to Bellingen. Forest, coastal heath, mostly near streams.

BEHAVIOUR: Stream-dweller. Egg clusters attached to vegetation in creek pool or permanent pond after spring/summer rain. ♂ calls from vegetation beside water.

CALL: Soft, high-pitched, quavering 'ik, ik, ik, iiii-k, iiii-k'.

GROWLING GRASS FROG *Litoria raniformis*

SIZE/ID: ♂ to 65mm, ♀ to 104mm. Green to dark green with dark golden-brown mottling, gold stripe along side, often with brown line below, pale green vertebral stripe in some. Back of thigh and groin turquoise. Skin with numerous broad tubercles. Small discs on digits, toes almost fully webbed.

HABITAT/RANGE: South-east Vic, SA and Tas. Woodland, grassy plains, urban fringes, lakes, floodplains.

BEHAVIOUR: Ground-dweller. Floating egg clumps in permanent ponds after spring/summer rain. ♂ calls while afloat.

CALL: Long, low-pitched, quavering growl.

WHIRRING TREE FROG *Litoria revelata*

SIZE/ID: ♂ to 28mm, ♀ to 36mm. Brown or grey-brown, ♂ yellow at night, with broad darker brown patch down back, upper lip pale. Back of thigh orange-red, groin yellow with black patches in northern form. Skin smooth. Discs on digits, fingers webbed at base, toes 3/4 webbed.

HABITAT/RANGE: Eastern NSW to Eungella, Qld. Forest, heath and swamps.

BEHAVIOUR: Tree-dweller. Eggs laid singly, attached to vegetation in permanent ponds after spring to autumn rain. ♂ calls from reed or leaf above water.

CALL: Rapid series of high-pitched whirring 'reet-reet' notes.

COMMON MIST FROG *Litoria rheocola*

SIZE/ID: ♂ to 38mm, ♀ to 43mm. Shades of brown, grey to olive or reddish, some with diffuse darker mottling. Many have a broad slightly darker patch between eyes to back. Skin with fine tubercles. Broad discs on digits, fingers 1/3 webbed, toes almost fully webbed.

HABITAT/RANGE: Endangered. North Qld Wet Tropics. Forest and rainforest near flowing streams.

BEHAVIOUR: Stream-dweller. White eggs laid in clump under rock in shallow part of stream. ♂ calls from vegetation by stream.

CALL: Single note with upward inflection repeated regularly.

ROTH'S TREE FROG *Litoria rothii*

SIZE/ID: ♂ to 48mm, ♀ to 57mm. Brown to grey, often with darker mottling. Armpit, groin and inner leg mottled black and yellow. Skin with small tubercles. Large discs on digits, fingers 1/3 webbed, toes almost fully webbed.

HABITAT/RANGE: South-east Qld to Cape York, northern Australia to Kimberleys. Woodland, swamps, agricultural and urban areas.

BEHAVIOUR: Tree-dweller. Eggs laid singly and in groups attached to vegetation in ponds or creek pools during spring/summer. ♂ calls from branch or ground.

CALL: Loud, distinctive series of about 5–6 notes, sounds like laughing.

64

RED TREE FROG *Litoria rubella*

SIZE/ID: ♂ to 37mm, ♀ to 43mm. Shades of red-brown to grey, broad dark stripe along sides. Some have darker flecks or mottling, others have broad darker band down back with lighter sides. Skin smooth. Broad discs on digits, toes about 1/2 webbed.

HABITAT/RANGE: Australia-wide except southern areas and Vic and Tas. Coast, woodland, swamps, floodplains, agricultural, urban and arid areas.

BEHAVIOUR: Tree-dweller. Floating egg clusters in ephemeral ponds after spring to autumn rain. ♂ calls from vegetation or ground.

CALL: Loud, continuous bleating sound.

GREEN-EYED TREE FROG *Litoria serrata*

SIZE/ID: ♂ to 54mm, ♀ to 85mm. Shades of red-brown, golden-brown or beige, often with darker mottling, some have green sheen. Upper half of eye green. Skin with numerous small to distinct tubercles. Large discs on digits, fingers 1/2 webbed, toes almost fully webbed.

HABITAT/RANGE: Qld Wet Tropics. Riparian forest and rainforest.

BEHAVIOUR: Stream-dweller. Egg clump attached beneath rock in shallow parts of stream from late winter to summer, often after rain. ♂ calls from fern or shrub by stream.

CALL: Series of soft clicks or 'tocs'.

SPENCER'S TREE FROG *Litoria spenceri*

SIZE/ID: ♂ to 41mm, ♀ to 52mm. Shades of green or brown, sometimes densely mottled. Green frogs may have gold or silver stripe on side. Inner leg and groin yellow. Skin with numerous distinct tubercles. Large discs on digits, toes fully webbed.

HABITAT/RANGE: Critically endangered. North-east Vic and one site in south-east NSW. Riparian forest above 300m.

BEHAVIOUR: Stream-dweller. Egg clump attached beneath rock in stream pool after spring/summer rain. ♂ calls from boulder or branch by stream.

CALL: Series of 6–7 clear notes.

MAGNIFICENT TREE FROG *Litoria splendida*

SIZE/ID: ♂ to 106mm, ♀ to 118mm. Green with whitish spots, yellow hands and feet and inner surfaces of limbs. Large raised glands over head and shoulders. Skin smooth. Large discs on digits, toes almost fully webbed.

HABITAT/RANGE: Kimberley, WA, just into far north-west NT. Rocky gorges and caves.

BEHAVIOUR: Feeds on anything smaller that moves, including small bats in the caves where it sometimes lives. Tree-dweller. Floating egg clusters in rock pools in summer wet season. ♂ calls from rock near water.

CALL: Loud, low-pitched 'crawk, crawk' similar to Green Tree Frog.

GLANDULAR TREE FROG *Litoria subglandulosa*

SIZE/ID: ♂ to 40mm, ♀ to 50mm. Green with broad gold stripe on side. Armpit, groin and inner leg yellow. White stripe along lip.

HABITAT/RANGE: Vulnerable. Ranges of north NSW and south-east Qld.

BEHAVIOUR: Egg clump attached to rock after spring/summer rain.

CALL: Five to seven 'or-āk' notes.

TORNIER'S FROG *Litoria tornieri*

SIZE/ID: ♂ to 34mm, ♀ to 36mm. Reddish to grey-brown with dark stripe on side of head. White bars (♀) or stripe (♂) on lip.

HABITAT/RANGE: Woodland, grassland and swamps in northern NT and WA.

BEHAVIOUR: Ground-dweller. Floating egg clumps in ponds after summer rain.

CALL: Loud, repeated, nasal 'quacking'.

TYLER'S TREE FROG *Litoria tyleri*

SIZE/ID: ♂ to 48mm, ♀ to 50mm. Brown, grey or yellow-brown with small green flecks, sometimes with faint darker markings. Armpit, groin and back of thigh yellow with dark mottling. Skin with fine tubercles. Large discs on digits, fingers 1/2 webbed, toes fully webbed.

HABITAT/RANGE: Coast and ranges south-east Qld, NSW to north-east Vic. Forest, swamps and farmland near permanent ponds.

BEHAVIOUR: Tree-dweller. Eggs laid singly or in small groups attached to vegetation in ponds after spring/summer rain. ♂ calls from branch or ground near water.

CALL: Loud laughing call of five short notes 'a-a-a-a-a'.

WHISTLING TREE FROG *Litoria verreauxii*

SIZE/ID: ♂ and ♀ to 36mm. Brown to beige with divided broad dark brown patch down back. Groin yellow with black spots, inner thigh reddish-orange. Skin smooth with very fine tubercles. Small discs on digits, toes 1/2 webbed. Endangered subspecies *L. v. alpina* often green with darker patches.

HABITAT/RANGE: Coast and ranges in south-east Qld, NSW to Vic. Forest, swamps, heath, alpine.

BEHAVIOUR: Tree-dweller. Small egg clusters attached to vegetation in pools after spring/summer rain.
♂ calls from low vegetation or ground near water.

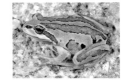

CALL: Series of rapid 'reet, reet, reet' notes.

Subspecies *L. v. alpina*.

WATJULUM ROCKET FROG *Litoria watjulumensis*

SIZE/ID: ♂ to 41mm, ♀ to 70mm. Brown to red-brown, broad dark stripe on side to mid-abdomen, ♂ yellow along side. Inner surface of leg yellow with indistinct mottling. Skin smooth. Small discs on digits, toes fully webbed.

HABITAT/RANGE: Northern WA, NT just into north-west Qld. Rocky escarpments and gorges near creeks.

BEHAVIOUR: Ground-dweller. Eggs laid in floating clumps in creek pools or flooded areas after summer rain. ♂ calls from rock or ground near water.

CALL: Long complex series of rapid 'chuck' notes merging into shrill, high-pitched rolling trill.

EASTERN STONY CREEK FROG *Litoria wilcoxii*

SIZE/ID: ♂ to 48mm, ♀ to 69mm. Grey to red-brown. ♂ yellow on side. Dark stripe from side of head. Groin/inner leg yellow, white or blue, spotted black.

HABITAT/RANGE: Creeks. South-east Qld to north of Sydney.

BEHAVIOUR: Egg clump on rock in creek pool after rain.

CALL: Soft, purring trill.

ORANGE-THIGHED TREE FROG *Litoria xanthomera*

SIZE/ID: ♂ to 56mm, ♀ to 85mm. Green with yellow sides, hands, feet and vocal sac. Large orange-red eye. Groin and inner leg orange.

HABITAT/RANGE: Rainforest in north Qld.

BEHAVIOUR: Tree-dweller.
Egg clusters in ephemeral ponds after rain.

CALL: Series of wavering moans ending with short, high-pitched trills.

TUSKED FROG *Adelotus brevis*

SIZE/ID: ♂ to 44mm, ♀ to 38mm. Dark grey to dark brown, dark patch between eyes and scattered dark patches. Groin and inner surfaces of legs red and black, belly marbled black and white. Skin rough with tubercles and ridges. Toes webbed at base.

HABITAT/RANGE: Coast and ranges from Eungella, Qld, to Gosford, NSW. Streams and permanent ponds in wet and dry forests.

BEHAVIOUR: Breeds after spring/summer rain. Foam nest of white eggs under vegetation or log. ♂ calls hidden at edge of pool.

CALL: Soft, high-pitched 'g-look' repeated day and night.

WESTERN SPOTTED FROG
Heleioporus albopunctatus

SIZE/ID: ♂ to 79mm, ♀ to 100mm. Maroon-brown with distinct white spots. White lip stripe. Large silver-grey eyes. Skin granular. Toes webbed at base.

HABITAT/RANGE: South-west Australia. Woodland, forest and wheatbelt areas near ponds and creeks.

BEHAVIOUR: Burrower, breeds before autumn rains. Foam nest of white eggs concealed in moist burrow in bank of pond or creek later to be flooded. Tadpoles develop in water. ♂ calls from burrow.

CALL: Soft, high-pitched 'ooo-ooo' with upward inflection, whistle-like quality.

GIANT BURROWING FROG
Heleioporus australiacus

SIZE/ID: ♂ to 78mm, ♀ to 97mm. Dark grey-brown to black, yellow spots on sides and sometimes limbs, eyes grey. Cream ridge from upper lip beyond ear. Skin granular. Toes webbed at base.

HABITAT/RANGE: Vulnerable. Coast and ranges of south-east Australia, from Sydney to north-east Vic. Heath, bushland, forests in sandy/clay soil.

BEHAVIOUR: Burrower, breeds after autumn or spring rains. Foam nest of white/grey eggs concealed in moist burrow or vegetation above water, later to be flooded. Tadpoles develop in water. ♂ calls from or near burrow.

CALL: Soft, high-pitched, owl-like 'oo-oo'.

HOOTING FROG *Heleioporus barycragus*

SIZE/ID: ♂ to 83mm, ♀ to 86mm. Dark grey-brown to almost black, yellow spots and patches over snout, sides and limbs. Yellow ridge from upper lip to past ear. Large silver-grey eyes. Skin granular. Toes about 1/3 webbed.

HABITAT/RANGE: Coast and ranges south-west Australia. Forests in sandy/clay soil areas near ephemeral wetlands.

BEHAVIOUR: Burrower, breeds after autumn or spring rains. Foam nest of white eggs in moist burrow near dry creek bed or pond, later to be flooded. Tadpoles develop in water. ♂ calls from burrow.

CALL: Repeated, single, fairly high-pitched note 'whooo...'.

MOANING FROG *Heleioporus eyrei*

SIZE/ID: ♂ to 66mm, ♀ to 63mm. Grey to brown with diffuse darker or paler mottling and pale band down front of snout. Large silver eyes. Skin granular. Toes webbed at base.

HABITAT/RANGE: Coast and ranges in south-west Australia. Forests in sandy/clay soil areas near ephemeral creeks or swamps.

BEHAVIOUR: Burrower, breeds before autumn rains. Foam nest of white eggs in moist burrow in bank of pond, later to be flooded. Tadpoles develop in water. ♂ calls from burrow.

CALL: High-pitched drawn-out moan with upward inflection 'ooooo'.

WHOOPING FROG *Heleioporus inornatus*

SIZE/ID: ♂ to 64mm, ♀ to 73mm. Dark grey-brown to brown, usually with paler mottling. Large silver-grey eyes. Skin granular. Toes webbed at base.

HABITAT/RANGE: Coast to ranges in south-west Australia. Forests and swamps in sandy/peat soil, often near ephemeral creek lines.

BEHAVIOUR: Burrower, breeds before autumn rains. Foam nest of white eggs in moist burrow in soil near dry water course or swamp, later to be flooded. Tadpoles develop in water. ♂ calls from burrow.

CALL: High-pitched drawn-out moan with upward inflection 'ooooo'.

SAND FROG *Heleioporus psammophilus*

SIZE/ID: ♂ to 62mm, ♀ to 60mm. Grey-brown with white or pale yellow marbling, pale band down snout. Large silver-grey eyes. Skin granular. Toes webbed at base.

HABITAT/RANGE: Coast and ranges in south-west Australia. Forests and swamps in sandy/clay soil areas, often near ephemeral ponds and creeks.

BEHAVIOUR: Burrower, breeds before autumn rains. Foam nest of white eggs in moist burrow near pond or swamp, later to be flooded. Tadpoles develop in water. ♂ calls from burrow.

CALL: Rapidly repeated high-pitched chirp sounding like a cricket.

FLETCHER'S FROG *Lechriodus fletcheri*

SIZE/ID: ♂ to 48mm, ♀ to 54mm. Yellow, brown or red-brown often with darker patches. Dark stripe on side of head, limbs banded. Skin granular with long folds. Toes webbed at base.

HABITAT/RANGE: Coast and ranges from south-east Qld to north of Sydney, NSW. Rainforest and wet sclerophyll forest.

BEHAVIOUR: Floating foam nest of eggs after spring/summer rain in small ephemeral pools and creek pools. ♂ calls from ground near water.

CALL: Soft, low-pitched, purring 'b-r-r-rt' repeated a few seconds apart.

MARBLED FROG *Limnodynastes convexiusculus*

SIZE/ID: ♂ to 58mm, ♀ to 61mm. Brown with numerous contrasting dark blotches and patches. White ridge from eye to arm and pale bars down upper lip. Skin granular, most raised blotches wart-like. Toes webbed at base.

HABITAT/RANGE: Across north Australia from Cape York, Qld, to Kimberley, WA. Savannah woodland and grassland.

BEHAVIOUR: Floating foam nest of eggs after spring/summer rain in ponds, swamps and flooded grassland. ♂ calls from vegetation in or near water.

CALL: Loud, continuous, high-pitched piping notes.

FLAT-HEADED FROG *Limnodynastes depressus*

SIZE/ID: ♂ to 54mm, ♀ to 50mm. Brown with numerous contrasting dark brown blotches and patches all over body and limbs. Flattened head with projecting rounded snout. Cream ridge from eye to arm. Skin granular. Toes webbed at base.

HABITAT/RANGE: Restricted to eastern Kimberley, WA, just into north-west NT. Lowland swampy grassland in clay soil areas.

BEHAVIOUR: Floating foam nest of eggs in summer at edge of billabongs, swamps and even in small puddles from cow hooves in grassland. ♂ calls from vegetation or near water.

CALL: A short rattling sound repeated regularly.

WESTERN BANJO FROG *Limnodynastes dorsalis*

SIZE/ID: ♂ to 64mm, ♀ to 73mm. Dark to pale brown with dark brown patches and spots and thin cream vertebral line. Dark stripe on side of head through eye. Groin and inner-leg red with black marbling. Skin with low tubercles. Toes webbed at base.

HABITAT/RANGE: Widespread in south-west WA. Coast to wheatbelt, woodland and forest.

BEHAVIOUR: Emerges from burrow after winter/spring rain. Floating foam nest of eggs among vegetation at sides of permanent ponds, swamps and stream pools. ♂ calls hidden in aquatic vegetation.

CALL: Loud 'bonk' repeated at intervals.

SOUTH-EASTERN BANJO FROG
Limnodynastes dumerilii dumerilii

SIZE/ID: ♂ to 70mm, ♀ to 73mm. Brown to grey-brown, cream ridge beneath eye and broad gland above arm. Side of body often rusty-orange, belly may be marbled with yellow. Skin granular. Large gland on leg, toes 1/4 webbed.

HABITAT/RANGE: Coast to ranges to inland south-east Qld, NSW, Vic and SA. Woodland, forest, heathland, grassland.

BEHAVIOUR: Burrower, emerges after heavy rain in spring to autumn. Floating foam nest of eggs among vegetation at sides of ponds and stream pools. ♂ calls hidden in aquatic vegetation.

CALL: Loud, explosive 'bonk'.

EASTERN BANJO FROG
Limnodynastes dumerilii grayi

SIZE/ID: ♂ to 60mm, ♀ to 55mm. Brown to light brown with darker patches, pale vertebral line. Cream ridge beneath eye to above arm. Sides of body may be rusty-brown. Skin smooth to finely granular. Large gland on leg, toes webbed at base.

HABITAT/RANGE: Coastal NSW, Nambucca south to Jervis Bay. Swamps in forest and heathland.

BEHAVIOUR: Burrower, emerges in spring to autumn after rain. Floating foam nest of eggs among vegetation at sides of ponds or swamps. ♂ calls while afloat among aquatic vegetation.

CALL: Loud, explosive 'bonk' repeated at intervals.

BARKING FROG *Limnodynastes fletcheri*

SIZE/ID: ♂ to 46mm, ♀ to 55mm. Brown to grey with darker patches, eyelids may have reddish tinge. Broad dark stripe on side of head to arm, cream to orange ridge from beneath eye to arm. Skin granular. Toes webbed at base.

HABITAT/RANGE: Mostly inland Qld, NSW, Vic, and just into SA. Woodland, grassland, swamps, river floodplains.

BEHAVIOUR: Breeds after heavy rain in spring to autumn. Floating foam nest of eggs among vegetation in ponds and swamps. ♂ calls among aquatic vegetation.

CALL: Short, low-pitched 'whuk' like a dog bark.

GIANT BANJO FROG *Limnodynastes interioris*

SIZE/ID: ♂ to 90mm, ♀ to 88mm. Beige to brown with darker patches, broad dark stripe on side of head. Orange over sides and legs, yellow beneath. Skin granular. Large orange gland on tibia, toes about 1/2 webbed.

HABITAT/RANGE: Inland NSW to northern Vic. Mallee, woodland or semi-arid areas in sandy-clay.

BEHAVIOUR: Burrower, emerges to breed after rain in spring to autumn. Floating foam nest of eggs among vegetation in ponds or stream pools. ♂ calls from aquatic vegetation, or from burrow.

CALL: Loud, resonant 'bonk'.

WOODWORKER FROG *Limnodynastes lignarius*

SIZE/ID: ♂ to 62mm, ♀ to 61mm. Dark brown with paler mottling or beige with darker mottling. White ridge beneath eye to arm. Very large tympanum. Skin granular with numerous tiny black spines. Toes webbed at base.

HABITAT/RANGE: Northern WA and NT. Rocky creeks, often in escarpments and gorges.

BEHAVIOUR: May burrow during dry, but lives in damp rock crevices in creeks when active. Breeds in summer wet season. Foam nest of white eggs in wet rock crevice, tadpoles develop in creeks. ♂ calls from within crevice.

CALL: Soft, repeated tapping sound.

STRIPED MARSH FROG *Limnodynastes peronii*

SIZE/ID: ♂ to 69mm, ♀ to 73mm. Brown with dark brown stripes and patches; some have a cream or salmon vertebral stripe. Dark stripe on side of head, cream or salmon ridge below eye to arm. Skin with smooth tubercles or ridges. Toes unwebbed.

HABITAT/RANGE: Coast and ranges of eastern Australia from north Qld to south-west Vic, just into SA and north Tas. Varied habitats.

BEHAVIOUR: Breeds after spring/summer rain. Floating foam nest of eggs in vegetation in ponds and creek pools. ♂ calls in water.

CALL: Short, continually repeated 'tok'.

SALMON-STRIPED FROG *Limnodynastes salmini*

SIZE/ID: ♂ to 76mm, ♀ to 61mm. Brown with dark brown stripes and patches, dark stripe on side of head, salmon ridge from below eye to arm. Salmon stripes and tinges on each side of body and on head. Skin with smooth tubercles and ridges. Toes with trace of webbing.

HABITAT/RANGE: Coast and inland south-east Qld and northern NSW. Woodland, grassland.

BEHAVIOUR: Breeds in spring to autumn after rain. Floating foam nest of eggs among vegetation in ponds, swamps or flooded grassland. ♂ calls from in or beside water.

CALL: Loud, short, repeated 'wuk'.

SPOTTED MARSH FROG
Limnodynastes tasmaniensis

SIZE/ID: ♂ to 42mm, ♀ to 47mm. Light grey-brown to olive-brown with dark blotches, may have cream vertebral stripe. Dark stripe on sides of head, cream ridge below eye to arm. Skin smooth or with low tubercles. Toes with trace of webbing.

HABITAT/RANGE: Coast and inland eastern Australia and Tasmania. Woodland, swamps, grassland, floodplains and urban fringes.

BEHAVIOUR: Breeds any time of year after rain. Small floating foam nest of eggs among vegetation in ponds, swamps or flooded grassland. ♂ calls while afloat.

CALL: Repeated rapid 'br-r-r-r-r-rt'.

NORTHERN BANJO FROG *Limnodynastes terrareginae*

SIZE/ID: ♂ to 76mm, ♀ to 79mm. Brown, sides yellow with black blotches. Groin and limbs red beneath. Dark stripe on side of head, cream ridge below eye to arm.

HABITAT/RANGE: Forest, swamps. Coast/ranges in Qld and north NSW.

BEHAVIOUR: Floating foam nest among vegetation after rain.

CALL: Short explosive 'bonk'.

SOUTHERN BARRED FROG *Mixophyes balbus*

SIZE/ID: ♂ to 65mm, ♀ to 100mm. Brown. Darker band down back. ♂ side yellow, darker stripes across limbs. Dark patches on snout. Eyes blue above pupil.

HABITAT/RANGE: Endangered. Forest. Coast and ranges of NSW and just into Vic.

BEHAVIOUR: Egg clump in shallow part of stream.

CALL: Soft, rapid low rattle.

CARBINE BARRED FROG *Mixophyes carbinensis*

SIZE/ID: ♂ to 72mm, ♀ to 78mm. Shades of brown, darker band and patches down back, dark stripes across limbs, cream spots on back of thighs. Black stripe on side of head, dark patches on snout. Large, dark brown eyes. Skin smooth. Toes almost fully webbed.

HABITAT/RANGE: Carbine and Windsor Tablelands, north Qld. Forest and rainforest.

BEHAVIOUR: Stream-dweller. Breeds in spring to summer after rain. Eggs flicked up onto bank above creek pool, hatchlings drop into water. ♂ calls on ground beside stream.

CALL: Loud, low-pitched 'wark, wark...'.

MOTTLED BARRED FROG *Mixophyes coggeri*

SIZE/ID: ♂ to 93mm, ♀ to 104mm. Red-brown to grey-brown, darker band and/or patches down back, dark spots over sides. Black stripe on side of head, dark patches on snout. Stripes across limbs, cream spots on back of thighs. Large, dark brown eyes. Skin smooth. Toes almost fully webbed.

HABITAT/RANGE: Ranges from Cooktown to Paluma, Qld. Forest and rainforest.

BEHAVIOUR: Stream-dweller. Breeds in summer to autumn after rain. Eggs flicked up onto bank above creek pool, hatchlings drop into water. ♂ calls on ground or rock by stream.

CALL: Deep, vibrating 'worg'.

GREAT BARRED FROG *Mixophyes fasciolatus*

SIZE/ID: ♂ to 65mm, ♀ to 101mm. Shades of brown to grey or yellowish, darker band and/or patches down back, small spots over sides, dark stripes across limbs. Black stripe on side of head. Large, dark brown eyes. Skin smooth. Toes almost fully webbed.

HABITAT/RANGE: Ranges from mid-eastern Qld to just south of Sydney, NSW. Forest and rainforest.

BEHAVIOUR: Stream-dweller. Breeds in spring to autumn after rain. Eggs flicked up onto bank above creek pool, hatchlings drop into water. ♂ calls on ground or rock by stream.

CALL: Low-pitched 'wark, wark...'.

FLEAY'S BARRED FROG *Mixophyes fleayi*

SIZE/ID: ♂ to 70mm, ♀ to 89mm. Brown to grey or reddish-brown, darker band and patches down back. Dark spots over sides, dark stripes across limbs. Narrow black stripe on side of head, dark patches on snout. Eyes large, blue-gold above pupil. Skin smooth. Toes about 1/2 webbed.

HABITAT/RANGE: Endangered, ranges of north-east NSW to south-east Qld. Forest and rainforest.

BEHAVIOUR: Stream-dweller. Breeds in winter to autumn after rain. Egg clump in shallow part of stream. ♂ calls on ground or rock by stream.

CALL: Loud 'ok-ok-ok...'.

GIANT BARRED FROG *Mixophyes iteratus*

SIZE/ID: ♂ to 78mm, ♀ to 115mm. Shades of brown or yellowish, darker band and patches down back, sides mottled yellow and black. Dark stripes across limbs, cream spots on back of thighs. Black stripe on side of head. Eyes gold above pupil. Skin smooth. Toes fully webbed.

HABITAT/RANGE: Coast and ranges south-east Qld to mid-eastern NSW. Forest and rainforest.

BEHAVIOUR: Stream-dweller. Breeds spring to autumn after rain. Eggs flicked up onto bank above creek pool, hatchlings drop into water. ♂ calls on ground or rock by stream.

CALL: Low-pitched guttural grunt or 'woh'.

NORTHERN BARRED FROG *Mixophyes schevilli*

SIZE/ID: ♂ to 75mm, ♀ to 92mm. Shades of brown, darker band and patches down back, sides pale, groin mottled dark. Dark stripes across limbs, cream spots on back of thighs. Black stripe on side of head, dark patches on snout. Large, dark brown eyes. Skin smooth. Toes almost fully webbed.

HABITAT/RANGE: Ranges from Atherton Tableland to Big Tableland, Qld. Forest and rainforest.

BEHAVIOUR: Stream-dweller. Breeds after spring/summer rain. Eggs flicked up onto bank above creek pool, hatchlings drop into water. ♂ calls on ground or rock by stream.

CALL: Loud, low-pitched 'wark, wark..'.

WHITE-FOOTED TRILLING FROG
Neobatrachus albipes

SIZE/ID: ♂ to 46mm, ♀ to 43mm. Shades of brown or grey, brown or olive marbling, some with pale vertebral line. Large silvery eyes. Skin mostly smooth, tiny spines on eyelids and tibia. Toes 3/4 webbed, large metatarsal tubercle.

HABITAT/RANGE: Southern to eastern south-west WA. Bushland and cleared areas, ponds, swamps, flooded areas.

BEHAVIOUR: Burrower, emerges to breed after spring or autumn rain. Eggs laid singly and small groups scattered among vegetation in pond. ♂ calls while afloat.

CALL: Fairly low-pitched rapid trill.

NORTHERN TRILLING FROG
Neobatrachus aquilonious

SIZE/ID: ♂ to 54mm, ♀ to 59mm. Brown to dark slate with yellow marbling all over body and limbs. Large silvery eyes. Skin with fine tubercles, tiny black spines on eyelids. Toes 1/2 webbed, large black metatarsal tubercle.

HABITAT/RANGE: Central arid WA with isolated populations in central NT. Claypans and other flooded water bodies.

BEHAVIOUR: Burrower, emerges to breed after heavy summer rain. Eggs in large floating clump. ♂ calls while afloat.

CALL: Soft, short, slow trill.

WHEATBELT FROG *Neobatrachus kunapalari*

SIZE/ID: ♂ to 58mm, ♀ to 61mm. Brown, grey or yellow with discrete dark blotches all over body and limbs. Large silvery eyes. ♂ with fine tubercles and tiny black spines, ♀ without spines. Toes about 3/4 webbed, large black metatarsal tubercle.

HABITAT/RANGE: Semi-arid south-west WA. Claypans and other flooded water bodies.

BEHAVIOUR: Burrower, emerges to breed any time after heavy rain. Eggs in large floating clump. ♂ calls while afloat.

CALL: Short high-pitched trill.

HUMMING FROG *Neobatrachus pelobatoides*

SIZE/ID: ♂ to 45mm, ♀ to 44mm. Smallest member of genus. Yellow-brown to grey with dark patches over body and limbs, cream vertebral stripe. Large silvery eyes. Skin with tubercles. Toes to 1/2 webbed, large metatarsal tubercle edged brown.

HABITAT/RANGE: South-west WA. Bushland, forest or farmland, temporary or semi-permanent ponds and water courses.

BEHAVIOUR: Burrower, emerges to breed after heavy rain, mainly in autumn. Eggs in floating clump. ♂ calls while afloat.

CALL: Low-pitched rapid trill.

PAINTED FROG *Neobatrachus pictus*

SIZE/ID: ♂ to 63mm, ♀ to 56mm. Brown, beige or yellow-brown with dark brown patches over body and limbs, cream vertebral stripe. Large silvery-bronze eyes. Skin with small tubercles, each with tiny spine in ♂. Toes almost fully webbed, large metatarsal tubercle edged with brown or black.

HABITAT/RANGE: Southern SA, Kangaroo Island and western Vic. Woodland to coastal and semi-arid areas, ponds, swamps and water courses.

BEHAVIOUR: Burrower, emerges to breed any time after heavy rain. Eggs in large floating clump. ♂ calls while afloat.

CALL: Long low-pitched trill.

SUDELL'S FROG *Neobatrachus sudellae*

SIZE/ID: ♂ to 50mm, ♀ to 55mm. Brown, grey or yellow-brown with dark brown patches or marbling all over body and limbs and a cream vertebral stripe (more so in eastern specimens). Large silvery-bronze eyes. Skin granular. Toes fully webbed, large black metatarsal tubercle.

HABITAT/RANGE: South-central to eastern Australia. Woodland to arid areas, ponds, swamps and water courses.

BEHAVIOUR: Burrower, emerges to breed any time after heavy rain. Eggs in large floating clump or attached to vegetation. ♂ calls while afloat.

CALL: Short musical trill.

SHOEMAKER FROG *Neobatrachus sutor*

SIZE/ID: ♂ to 45mm, ♀ to 51mm. Shades of brown or yellow with discrete dark blotches or spots all over body and limbs. Large silvery eyes. Skin smooth. Toes fully webbed, large black metatarsal tubercle.

HABITAT/RANGE: South-west WA to central Australia. Woodland, grassland to semi-arid areas, claypans and other flooded water bodies.

BEHAVIOUR: Burrower, emerges to breed mainly in summer to autumn after rain. Eggs in strings and small clusters on vegetation. ♂ calls in shallow water near edge of pond.

CALL: Series of short tapping, sounds like a shoemaker.

PLONKING FROG *Neobatrachus wilsmorei*

SIZE/ID: ♂ to 61mm, ♀ to 63mm. Dark brown to purple-brown with yellow vertebral stripe and other stripes and spots. Large silvery-gold eyes. Skin smooth. Toes 3/4 webbed, large black metatarsal tubercle.

HABITAT/RANGE: Semi-arid to arid areas of central western WA. Claypans and other large flooded water bodies.

BEHAVIOUR: Burrower, emerges to breed mainly in summer to autumn after heavy rain. Eggs entwined among vegetation. ♂ calls while afloat.

CALL: Repeated 'plonk, plonk...'.

CRUCIFIX FROG *Notaden bennetti*

SIZE/ID: ♂ to 63mm, ♀ to 68mm. Black and red tubercles form cross-shape on yellow or brown back. White, black and red spots over yellow to brown sides. Very short blunt snout. Skin with numerous tubercles, exudes gluey secretion. Toes 1/4 webbed.

HABITAT/RANGE: Semi-arid to arid areas of inland NSW and Qld. Woodland and swamps, temporary water bodies and floodplains.

BEHAVIOUR: Feeds on ants and termites. Burrower, emerges to breed mainly in summer to autumn after heavy rain. Eggs initially in foamy floating clump. ♂ calls in or near shallow water.

CALL: High-pitched, owl-like 'whoop, whoop...'.

NORTHERN SPADEFOOT *Notaden melanoscaphus*

SIZE/ID: ♂ to 54mm, ♀ to 60mm. Brownish with dark patches on back and side of head, divided darker bar down short blunt snout. Black inner metatarsal tubercle.

HABITAT/RANGE: Far north NT and WA. Savannah to semi-arid/stony areas.

BEHAVIOUR: Burrower. Breeds after summer rain. Floating egg clump. ♂ calls from shallow water.

CALL: High-pitched, owl-like 'whoop, whoop...'.

DESERT SPADEFOOT *Notaden nichollsi*

SIZE/ID: ♂ to 63mm, ♀ to about 67mm. Brown with orange spots, black tubercles and dark dorsal patches, white tubercles over sides. Brown patches on side of head. Very short, blunt snout.

HABITAT/RANGE: Central to north-west Australia. Desert and savannah.

BEHAVIOUR: Burrower. Breeds after summer rain. Floating egg clump. ♂ calls from shallow water.

CALL: High-pitched, owl-like 'whoop, whoop...'.

KIMBERLEY SPADEFOOT *Notaden weigeli*

SIZE/ID: ♂ to 79mm, ♀ to 80mm. Yellow-brown with orange-red spots, larger brown spots and white spots over sides. Snout and limbs darker with pale tubercles. Robust frog, very short blunt snout. Skin covered with rough tubercles. Toes webbed at base.

HABITAT/RANGE: North-west Kimberley region, WA. Rocky gorges and plateaus, rock pools and crevices in floodplains.

BEHAVIOUR: Often feeds on ants and termites. Burrower and rock-dweller, comes to surface to breed after heavy summer rain. Eggs unknown.

CALL: High-pitched, owl-like 'whoop, whoop...'.

BAW BAW FROG *Philoria frosti*

SIZE/ID: ♂ to 46mm, ♀ to 55mm. Dark brown to reddish-brown, some with mustard yellow areas. Large parotoid glands on shoulders. Skin with tubercles. Toes unwebbed.

HABITAT/RANGE: Critically endangered, restricted to small areas on Mt Baw Baw, Vic. Drainage lines in forest.

BEHAVIOUR: Breeds in moist soil deep beneath large rocks and moss in spring and summer. Large white eggs laid in small foamy clump in hidden mud nest, tadpoles develop in seepage areas. ♂ calls from nest site.

CALL: Low-pitched 'crok'.

MOUNTAIN FROG *Philoria kundagungan*

SIZE/ID: ♂ and ♀ to 28mm. Dark brown, red-brown, purple-red or yellow above, bright yellow beneath with red throat (♂). Some with dark stripe from side of head to arm. Skin smooth. Toes unwebbed.

HABITAT/RANGE: Threatened, restricted to small areas in ranges of northern NSW and south-east Qld. Drainage lines under rock and mossy vegetation in forest.

BEHAVIOUR: Breeds in moist soil beneath large rocks and moss in spring and summer. Large white eggs in small foamy clump in mud nest, tadpoles develop in seepage areas. ♂ calls from nest site.

CALL: Low-pitched guttural 'ork'.

LOVERIDGE'S MOUNTAIN FROG *Philoria loveridgei*

SIZE/ID: ♂ to 30mm, ♀ to 32mm. Brown or grey, often with broad dark patch over lower back, some with dark band over shoulders. Dark stripe on side. Skin with fine tubercles and long folds. Toes unwebbed.

HABITAT/RANGE: Endangered, restricted to small areas in ranges of northern NSW and south-east Qld. Drainage lines under rocks and mossy vegetation in forest.

BEHAVIOUR: Breeds in moist soil beneath large rocks in spring/summer. Large white eggs in small, non-foamy clump in mud nest, where tadpoles develop in broken-down jelly capsules. ♂ calls from nest site.

CALL: Very low-pitched short 'bork'.

SPHAGNUM FROG *Philoria sphagnicola*

SIZE/ID: ♂ to 35mm, ♀ to 37mm. Brown, red or yellow to almost black, darker flecks and patches, yellow patches or yellow band down back in some. Dark stripe on side of head. Skin with tubercles and folds. Toes unwebbed.

HABITAT/RANGE: Vulnerable, restricted to ranges of northern NSW. Drainage lines under rocks and mossy vegetation in forest.

BEHAVIOUR: Breeds in small soaks beneath large rocks in spring and summer. Large white eggs in small foamy clump in mud or mossy nest, tadpoles develop in seepage water. ♂ calls from nest site.

CALL: Very low-pitched resonant 'b-o-r-k'.

ORNATE BURROWING FROG
Platyplectrum ornatum

SIZE/ID: ♂ to 41mm, ♀ to 42mm. Brown, yellow or red-brown often with darker marbling, spots or patterns. Patches on side of head. Skin with tubercles. Toes webbed at base.

HABITAT/RANGE: Widespread across eastern and northern Australia. Coastal, woodland, grasslands and forest verges.

BEHAVIOUR: Breeds in temporary pools after rain in spring and summer. Eggs laid in flat, floating, foamy rafts. ♂ calls in shallow water.

CALL: Short, resonant 'unk'.

SPENCER'S BURROWING FROG
Platyplectrum spenceri

SIZE/ID: ♂ to 44mm, ♀ to 49mm. Shades of brown, grey or yellow with darker or lighter marbling. Stripe on snout to eyes, bars on side of head. Skin with tubercles, minute spines in ♂. Toes fully webbed.

HABITAT/RANGE: Widespread across central to mid-western Australia. Woodland, floodplains, ponds and creeks and rivers in gorges.

BEHAVIOUR: Breeds in temporary pools or flooded areas after rain in spring and summer. Eggs in flat, floating, foamy rafts. ♂ calls in shallow water.

CALL: Low-pitched rapid, repeated 'wuk-wuk-wuk...'

SANDHILL FROG *Arenophryne rotunda*

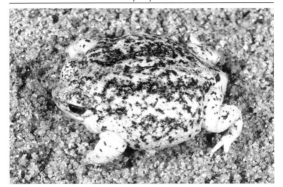

SIZE/ID: ♂ to 31mm, ♀ to 39mm. Pale grey to brown with darker patches and red spots. Thin cream vertebral stripe often tinged with reddish spots. Skin fairly smooth. Toes unwebbed.

HABITAT/RANGE: Small area from Edel Land Peninsula to Shark Bay and Dirk Hartog Island, WA. Arid coastal sandhills.

BEHAVIOUR: Often feeds on ants. Front-end burrower. Breeds in damp sandy burrows to 1m beneath surface in autumn before heavy rain. Eggs large and white, no tadpole stage, embryos develop directly to tiny frogs within jelly capsule. ♂ calls from underground or at surface.

CALL: Short 'squelch'.

POUCHED FROG *Assa darlingtoni*

SIZE/ID: ♂ to 19mm, ♀ to 21mm. Brown, red, yellow or grey with darker patches or broad bands. Skin smooth to granular, ♂ with pouch slit on either side. Toes unwebbed.

HABITAT/RANGE: Ranges of northern NSW and south-east Qld in moist forest.

BEHAVIOUR: Unique breeding mode in spring/summer: large white eggs laid in moist nest under leaf litter, rocks or logs on forest floor. ♂ sits with eggs until hatched embryos wriggle into his pouches (see arrow above) and emerge three months later as tiny frogs. ♂ calls from leaf litter, log or rock.

CALL: String of rapid short notes.

MOSS FROGLET *Bryobatrachus nimbus*
(also known as *Crinia nimba*)

SIZE/ID: ♂ to 27mm, ♀ to 30mm. Shades of brown with pairs
of bilateral dark patches on back and usually a V-shaped
patch between eyes. Skin smooth to granular and some folds.
Toes unwebbed.

HABITAT/RANGE: Threatened. Known only from southern ranges in
Tas. Alpine moorland.

BEHAVIOUR: Breeds in clumps of moss, lichen or peat in spring/
summer. Eggs large and white, laid in nest in moss, hatched
embryos do not feed, develop in broken-down jelly capsules.
♂ calls beneath surface in nest chamber.

CALL: String of rapid clicks.

BILINGUAL FROGLET *Crinia bilingua*

SIZE/ID: ♂ to 23mm. ♀ to 20mm. Grey, yellow-brown or red-brown with darker lyre-shaped ridges, patches and spots, often a broad triangular patch between eyes. Skin granular often with some folds. Toes unwebbed.

HABITAT/RANGE: Far northern NT and WA. Savannah woodland, floodplains, swamps and rocky creeks.

BEHAVIOUR: Breeds in temporary water in summer wet season. Eggs very small, laid singly and attached to vegetation. ♂ calls from vegetation in or near shallow water.

CALL: Low-pitched two-note call, one short note (not always used) and one longer 'rattle'.

DESERT FROGLET *Crinia deserticola*

SIZE/ID: ♂ to 18mm, ♀ to 20mm. Grey, beige, brown, olive-green or reddish, with darker triangle between eyes, X-shaped patch behind eyes and other patches, bands across legs. Skin smooth to granular. Toes unwebbed.

HABITAT/RANGE: Northern coastal and central NT, Qld and NSW. Grassland, swamps and floodplains, often in black soil areas.

BEHAVIOUR: Breeds in temporary water after spring/summer rain. Eggs very small, laid singly, most attached to vegetation. ♂ calls from vegetation in or near shallow water.

CALL: High-pitched 'chirrup'.

NORTHERN FLINDERS RANGES FROGLET
Crinia flindersensis

SIZE/ID: ♂ to 21mm, ♀ to 26mm. Shades of brown with or without darker lyrate patch or stripes and other patches, bands across legs. Skin smooth to granular. Toes unwebbed.

HABITAT/RANGE: Northern Flinders Ranges, SA. Rocky or sandy creeks in gorges.

BEHAVIOUR: Breeds in creek pools opportunistically after rain, mostly in late winter to spring. Eggs laid in adherent clump attached to underside of partly submerged rocks.

CALL: Unknown.

QUACKING FROGLET *Crinia georgiana*

SIZE/ID: ♂ to 44mm, ♀ to 41mm. Our largest *Crinia* species, ♂ bigger than ♀. Shades of brown, beige or grey, variable darker patches, stripes or mottling, thin cream vertebral line in some. Red in groin and armpits. Skin smooth to granular. Toes unwebbed.

HABITAT/RANGE: South-west WA. Forest and lowland coastal areas, creek lines and seepage areas.

BEHAVIOUR: Breeds in temporary water from autumn to spring after rain. Eggs quite large, laid singly over substrate. ♂ calls from tussock or under rock near pool.

CALL: Three note 'quack, quack, quack'.

CLICKING FROGLET *Crinia glauerti*

SIZE/ID: ♂ to 23mm, ♀ to 24mm. Shades of brown, grey or almost black, often with stripes, lyrate markings or patches. Skin smooth to granular, some with longitudinal folds. Toes unwebbed.

HABITAT/RANGE: South-west WA. Forests to coastal woodland, creeks, swamps or pools.

BEHAVIOUR: Breeds in creeks or isolated pools opportunistically after rain. Eggs laid singly, attached to vegetation. ♂ calls near water, partly hidden.

CALL: Low-pitched, rapid clicking or metallic rattling.

BLEATING FROGLET *Crinia pseudinsignifera*

SIZE/ID: ♂ to 25mm, ♀ to 29mm. Shades of brown or grey mostly with stripes, lyrate markings or patches. Skin smooth to granular, some with longitudinal folds. Toes unwebbed.

HABITAT/RANGE: South-west WA. Rocky plateaus, usually in granite forest.

BEHAVIOUR: Breeds in creeks, swamps or isolated rock pools opportunistically after winter/spring rain. Eggs laid singly attached to rock or leaf litter. ♂ calls in or near shallow water.

CALL: Three or four high-pitched 'bleating' notes.

SOUTHERN FLINDERS RANGES FROGLET
Crinia riparia

SIZE/ID: ♂ to 22mm, ♀ to 25mm. Shades of brown or grey with or without darker lyrate patch or stripes and other patches. Bands across legs. Skin smooth to granular. Toes unwebbed.

HABITAT/RANGE: Southern part of Flinders Ranges, SA. Rocky streams, or creeks in gorges.

BEHAVIOUR: Breeds in rock pools in creeks opportunistically after rain, mostly in winter to spring. Eggs laid in adherent clump attached to underside of partly submerged rocks. ♂ calls near or in shallow water.

CALL: Long, harsh 'kr-a-a-a-ack'.

COMMON EASTERN FROGLET *Crinia signifera*

SIZE/ID: ♂ to 25mm, ♀ to 29mm. Brown, yellow or grey mostly with stripes, lyrate markings or patches. Skin smooth to granular, some with longitudinal folds. Belly and legs heavily mottled white and black. Toes unwebbed.

HABITAT/RANGE: Widespread in south-east Australia. Alpine to ranges and coastal regions, woodland, forest, heath and swamps.

BEHAVIOUR: Breeds in small isolated water bodies or creeks and swamps after rain, mainly in autumn to spring. Eggs laid singly, attached to vegetation or substrate. ♂ calls from vegetation in shallow water.

CALL: Low-pitched 'crick' repeated continuously.

SLOANE'S FROGLET *Crinia sloanei*

SIZE/ID: ♂ to 16mm, ♀ to 18mm. Grey, olive to mustard-yellow with slightly darker lyrate markings and reddish tinges in some. Skin smooth to granular, some with ridges. Toes unwebbed.

HABITAT/RANGE: Threatened species, now restricted to south-eastern Murray River valley. Woodland, swamps, grassland and agricultural areas.

BEHAVIOUR: Breeds in pools or swamps after rain in winter to spring. Eggs laid singly, attached to vegetation or substrate. ♂ calls among vegetation in shallow water.

CALL: Short nasal 'chick' repeated continuously.

TASMANIAN FROGLET *Crinia tasmaniensis*

SIZE/ID: ♂ to 23mm, ♀ to 29mm. Brown, grey, rusty-red or olive-brown with darker lyrate patches and other markings, sometimes a cream vertebral stripe. Belly and underside of limbs pink to red. Skin mostly granular with some with ridges. Toes unwebbed.

HABITAT/RANGE: Widespread across Tas from ranges to coast. Rocky creeks, ponds, swamps and soaks in forest or coastal heath.

BEHAVIOUR: Breeds in shallow water after rain in spring and summer. Eggs laid in small clumps on substrate. ♂ calls hidden beside water.

CALL: Strident, quavering 'bleat'.

WALLUM FROGLET *Crinia tinnula*

SIZE/ID: ♂ and ♀ to 18mm. Shades of brown, yellow or grey mostly with stripes, lyrate markings or patches. Skin smooth to granular, some with longitudinal folds. Belly has white cross and darker mottling. Toes unwebbed.

HABITAT/RANGE: Threatened species. South-east Qld and NSW to Sydney, coastal wallum swamps and heathland.

BEHAVIOUR: Breeds in shallow water after rain, mainly from autumn to spring. Eggs laid singly, attached to vegetation. ♂ calls hidden beside water or while afloat.

CALL: High-pitched 'chick, chick, chick' and two-note tag 'ke-chik, ke-chik'.

WHITE-BELLIED FROG *Geocrinia alba*

SIZE/ID: ♂ and ♀ to 25mm. Brown to grey-brown with white belly. Juvenile has dark belly speckled blue. Skin granular with prominent darker tubercles. Toes unwebbed.

HABITAT/RANGE: Critically endangered. Only in very small area near Witchcliffe, south-west WA. Forest in peaty soil.

BEHAVIOUR: Breeds in small seepage areas near creeks after rain, from late winter to early summer. Large white eggs laid in moist, hidden mud basin on land, tiny tadpoles develop in broken-down jelly capsules. ♂ calls hidden beneath vegetation.

CALL: Low-pitched string of rapid 'tick, tick...' clicks.

TASMANIAN SMOOTH FROG *Geocrinia laevis*

SIZE/ID: ♂ to 27mm, ♀ to 35mm. Brown, grey or reddish, faint darker patch between eyes and divided patch down back. Dark stripe and patches on side of head. Belly white with dark spots, ♂ with yellow throat. Skin with tubercles. Toes unwebbed.

HABITAT/RANGE: Tas, King Island, south-west Vic. Forest, woodland.

BEHAVIOUR: Eggs laid on land in adherent chain under vegetation

or leaf litter in autumn, in site later to be flooded. Tadpoles develop in water of pools. ♂ calls hidden beneath vegetation.

CALL: Low-pitched rasp.

TICKING FROG *Geocrinia leai*

SIZE/ID: ♂ to 21mm, ♀ to 26mm. Brown, grey or yellow-brown with broad darker patch down back, some with large yellow or small pale blue spots. Belly greenish-brown or translucent yellow. Skin smooth. Toes unwebbed.

HABITAT/RANGE: South-west WA. Mainly in forest.

BEHAVIOUR: Eggs laid on land in adherent clump under vegetation or leaf litter in autumn to spring, in site later to be flooded. Tadpoles develop in water of ponds, or pools of creeks or rivers. ♂ calls while hidden.

CALL: High-pitched 'chic, chic, chic...'.

WALPOLE FROG *Geocrinia lutea*

SIZE/ID: ♂ to 23mm, ♀ to 22mm. Brown with broad darker divided patch from between eyes down back. Belly white with yellow on legs. ♂ has black throat. Skin with tubercles. Toes unwebbed.

HABITAT/RANGE: South-west WA, Walpole to Nornalup north to Mt Frankland. Karri forest, swamps and near small creeks.

BEHAVIOUR: Large white eggs laid on land in moist hidden depressions in moss or peaty mud in spring. Tiny tadpoles develop

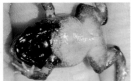

in broken-down jelly from capsules. ♂ calls hidden beneath vegetation.

CALL: Low-pitched string of metallic clicks.

ROSEATE FROG *Geocrinia rosea*

SIZE/ID: ♂ to 23mm, ♀ to 25mm. Brown or grey to almost black with broad slightly darker divided patch from between eyes down back. Belly pink, throat of ♂ pink and black. Skin with some tubercles. Toes unwebbed.

HABITAT/RANGE: South-west WA, near Pemberton and Dombakup. Karri forest, often near small creeks.

BEHAVIOUR: Large white eggs laid on land in moist hidden depressions in peaty mud in spring. Tiny tadpoles develop in broken-down jelly from capsules. ♂ calls hidden beneath vegetation.

CALL: Low-pitched string of metallic clicks, 'tick, tick, tick...'.

VICTORIAN SMOOTH FROG *Geocrinia victoriana*

SIZE/ID: ♂ to 28mm, ♀ to 33mm. Brown, grey or reddish, darker patch between eyes, variable spots and patches. Dark stripe on side of head in some. Belly white with dark spots, ♂ with yellow throat. Skin with tubercles. Toes unwebbed.

HABITAT/RANGE: Vic, Tas and south-east NSW. Forest, woodland, alpine, grassland. Creeks, swamps and ponds.

BEHAVIOUR: Eggs laid on land in adherent clump under vegetation

in late summer and autumn, in site later to be flooded. Tadpoles develop in water. ♂ calls hidden beneath vegetation.

CALL: In two parts – a lower note followed high-pitched 'pips'.

136

ORANGE-BELLIED FROG *Geocrinia vitellina*

SIZE/ID: ♂ and ♀ to 25mm. Brown or grey with broad darker divided patch from between eyes down back. Belly bright orange-yellow. Skin with prominent tubercles. Toes unwebbed.

HABITAT/RANGE: Critically endangered, south-west WA, near Witchcliffe. Remnant forest, near creeks.

BEHAVIOUR: Large white eggs laid on land in moist hidden depressions in peaty mud in spring. Tiny tadpoles develop in broken-down jelly from capsules. ♂ calls hidden beneath vegetation.

CALL: Low-pitched string of rapid clicks, 'tick, tick, tick...'.

FOREST TOADLET *Metacrinia nichollsi*

SIZE/ID: ♂ to 21mm, ♀ to 28mm. Brown or grey to almost black, scattered darker flecks in some. Belly mottled black and white with yellow patches. Skin with prominent tubercles. Toes unwebbed.

HABITAT/RANGE: South-west WA, around Pemberton to Walpole. Karri and Jarrah forest.

BEHAVIOUR: Large white eggs laid on land in nest site under logs, leaf litter or rocks prior to winter rain. No tadpole stage – eggs

develop directly into tiny frogs within the jelly capsule. ♂ calls from hidden nest site and may remain near eggs during development period.

CALL: Low-pitched single note.

TURTLE FROG *Myobatrachus gouldii*

SIZE/ID: ♂ to 42mm, ♀ to 51mm. Grey-brown to pinkish-brown with faint or distinct darker mottling. Very small head and eyes, muscular arms. Skin smooth. Fingers short and broad. Toes unwebbed.

HABITAT/RANGE: South-west WA, Kalbarri to Esperance. Dry coastal to arid areas in sandy soil.

BEHAVIOUR: Favours termites and ants. Front-end burrower. ♂ calls on surface in spring and leads ♀ into deep burrow where very large white eggs are laid in damp sand cavity in autumn, prior to winter rain. No tadpole stage, eggs develop directly into frogs within jelly capsule.

CALL: Series of abrupt, deep croaks.

HASWELL'S FROG *Paracrinia haswelli*

SIZE/ID: ♂ to 33mm, ♀ to 35mm. Brown or grey-brown with thin cream vertebral line. Dark stripe on side of head to arm, red in armpits, groin and back of thighs. Skin smooth to finely granular. Toes unwebbed.

HABITAT/RANGE: South-east coastal Australia, NSW to Vic. Woodland, forest and heath from coast to adjacent plateaus. Swamps and ponds.

BEHAVIOUR: Eggs laid in clumps attached to vegetation in pools after autumn/spring rain. ♂ calls from ground near or in water.

CALL: Short, nasal, penetrating 'neep'.

RED-CROWNED TOADLET *Pseudophryne australis*

SIZE/ID: ♂ to 28mm, ♀ to 30mm. Dark grey, bright orange-red crown and stripe on lower back. Variable red and black blotches over back. Undersurface black and white. Skin finely granular. Toes unwebbed.

HABITAT/RANGE: Vulnerable, restricted to Sydney Basin, NSW. Sandstone bushland and heath. Ephemeral creek lines.

BEHAVIOUR: Eats ants and termites. Large eggs laid on land at any time of year, in damp nest beneath rock or leaf litter beside creek pool. Tadpoles develop in water. ♂ calls from nest near water and remains with eggs.

CALL: Nasal, penetrating 'nee-ak'.

BIBRON'S TOADLET *Pseudophryne bibroni*

SIZE/ID: ♂ to 30mm, ♀ to 32mm. Dark grey or brown, variable dark patches and spots, may have faint orange crown and stripe on lower back, buff or yellow upper arms. Undersurface black and white. Skin granular. Toes unwebbed.

HABITAT/RANGE: South-east Qld, NSW, Vic and SA. Forest, grassland and swamps.

BEHAVIOUR: Often feeds on ants. Large eggs laid on land any time
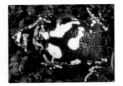
after rain, in damp nest beneath vegetation beside water. Tadpoles develop in water. ♂ calls from nest near water and remains with eggs.

CALL: Nasal, penetrating 'neep'.

RED-BACKED TOADLET *Pseudophryne coriacea*

SIZE/ID: ♂ to 24mm, ♀ to 27mm. Dark grey to brown with red-brown or orange-red back, dark stripe on side of head and body. Undersurface black and white. Skin finely granular. Toes unwebbed.

HABITAT/RANGE: South-east Qld to mid-eastern NSW. Forest and adjacent land, ephemeral creek lines.

BEHAVIOUR: Favours ants. Large eggs laid on land at any time after rain, in damp nest beneath rock or vegetation near water. Tadpoles develop in water. ♂ calls from nest near water and stays with eggs.

CALL: Nasal, penetrating 'neep'.

SOUTHERN CORROBOREE FROG
Pseudophryne corroboree

SIZE/ID: ♂ to 29mm, ♀ to 31mm. Bright yellow and black stripes, each frog with individual pattern. Undersurface black and white. Skin smoothly undulating. Toes unwebbed.

HABITAT/RANGE: Critically endangered, reduced to one site at Mt Kosciuszko NP, NSW. Sphagnum bogs near creek pools. Captive-bred frogs from zoos have been released at controlled sites in habitat.

BEHAVIOUR: Favours ants. Large eggs laid in summer in damp moss cavity, near pools or bogs later to be flooded. Tadpoles develop in water. ♂ calls from nest near water and remains with eggs.

CALL: Nasal, penetrating 'wrank'.

MAGNIFICENT TOADLET
Pseudophryne covacevichae

SIZE/ID: ♂ and ♀ to 28mm. Dark grey-brown with red-brown over back, yellow stripe on lower back, upper arms and vent yellow. Undersurface black and white. Skin with dark tubercles. Toes unwebbed.

HABITAT/RANGE: Vulnerable, north Qld near Ravenshoe. Forest, ephemeral creek lines.

BEHAVIOUR: Often feeds on ants. Large eggs laid after summer rain, in damp nest under vegetation or rock above pool. Tadpoles develop in water. ♂ calls from nest near water and stays with eggs.

CALL: Nasal, penetrating 'neep'.

GÜNTHER'S TOADLET *Pseudophryne guentheri*

SIZE/ID: ♂ to 30mm, ♀ to 33mm. Grey or brown, variable paler buff patches, reddish tinges and stripe on lower back in some. Belly white with small dark patches, throat brown in ♂. Skin with tubercles and folds. Toes unwebbed.

HABITAT/RANGE: South-west WA. Forest, swamps, ephemeral pools.

BEHAVIOUR: Often feeds on ants. Large eggs laid on land in autumn, in damp nest inside tunnel, in areas likely to be flooded. Tadpoles develop in water. ♂ calls from nest and remains with eggs.

CALL: Nasal rasp or squelch.

LARGE TOADLET *Pseudophryne major*

SIZE/ID: ♂ to 29mm, ♀ to 31mm. Grey, buff or brown, variable darker patches or red-brown wash over back. Yellow upper arms. Undersurface black and white. Skin with tubercles and folds. Toes unwebbed.

HABITAT/RANGE: South-east Qld north to near Townsville. Forest, swamps, woodland, heath, grassland.

BEHAVIOUR: Often feeds on ants. Large eggs laid on land from autumn to spring, in damp nest beneath vegetation or logs, in areas later to be flooded. Tadpoles develop in water. ♂ calls from nest site and stays with eggs.

CALL: Nasal 'ratchet'-like sound.

NORTHERN CORROBOREE FROG
Pseudophryne pengilleyi

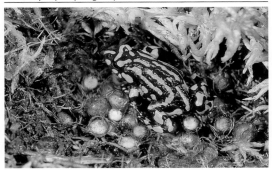

SIZE/ID: ♂ and ♀ to 27mm. Greenish-yellow and black stripes all over, each frog with individual pattern. Undersurface black and white. Skin smoothly undulating. Toes unwebbed.

HABITAT/RANGE: Critically endangered. ACT and NSW. Restricted to a few sites in Brindabella and Fiery Ranges. Montane forest, heath, sphagnum bogs.

BEHAVIOUR: Favours ants. Large eggs laid on land from summer to early autumn, in damp nest beneath moss or logs, in areas likely to be flooded. Tadpoles develop in water. ♂ calls from nest site and remains with eggs.

CALL: Nasal penetrating 'wrank'.

SOUTHERN TOADLET
Pseudophryne semimarmorata

SIZE/ID: ♂ to 28mm, ♀ to 35mm. Grey or brown with distinct dark tubercles. Upper arms, front and back of thighs and belly orange-yellow, often with black and white patches on belly. Toes unwebbed.

HABITAT/RANGE: Southern Vic and eastern Tas. Forest, grassland and swamps.

BEHAVIOUR: Often feeds on ants. Large eggs laid on land in damp burrow beneath vegetation or logs in summer to early autumn, in areas likely to be flooded. Tadpoles develop in water. ♂ calls from nest and stays with eggs.

CALL: Short, resonant 'creek'.

SOUTHERN GASTRIC BROODING FROG
Rheobatrachus silus

SIZE/ID: ♂ to 44mm, ♀ to 57mm. Dark brown to black with diffuse darker and lighter patches. Dark streak from eye to arm. Eyes very large and elevated on head. Belly white, legs yellow beneath. Digits claw-like, toes fully webbed.

HABITAT/RANGE: South-east Qld. Presumed extinct, once known only from Conondale and Blackhall Ranges. Closely related to Northern Gastric Brooding Frog, also presumed extinct. Rivers in forest.

BEHAVIOUR: Aquatic. Fertilised eggs develop from tadpole to frog in stomach of ♀, regurgitated as froglets. ♂ calls from rock crevice above or near water.

CALL: Loud, low-pitched 'wark'.

SUNSET FROG *Spicospina flammocaerulea*

SIZE/ID: ♂ to 35mm, ♀ to 36mm. Grey to brown. Groin, beneath limbs and much of belly mottled iridescent blue and black. Hands, feet, armpits, cloacal region and remainder of undersurface yellow-orange. Skin with numerous raised tubercles. Toes unwebbed.

HABITAT/RANGE: Endangered, south-west WA. Fragmented populations in high-rainfall areas mainly near Walpole. Forest in acid swamp areas.

BEHAVIOUR: Eggs laid singly within thick algae mats in deep pools in spring. ♂ calls from algae mat or beside pool.

CALL: Rapid, two-note 'da-duk'.

EUNGELLA DAY FROG *Taudactylus eungellensis*

SIZE/ID: ♂ to 28mm, ♀ to 36mm. Yellow or greenish-brown to brown with variable darker patches, dark stripe from eye to arm, bands across limbs. Slender body, long legs. Skin granular. Fingers and toes with expanded discs. Toes unwebbed.

HABITAT/RANGE: Critically endangered. Restricted to a few populations in Clarke Range near Eungella, Qld. Rainforest streams.

BEHAVIOUR: White eggs laid in clump under rock in stream from spring to autumn after rain. ♂ calls from rock near water.

CALL: Soft chirping sound.

LIEM'S TINKER FROG *Taudactylus liemi*

SIZE/ID: ♂ to 26mm, ♀ to 29mm. Dark brown to yellow or reddish-brown with darker markings. Dark stripe on side of head, bands across limbs. Skin granular. Fingers and toes with very small discs. Toes unwebbed.

HABITAT/RANGE: Near threatened. Restricted to upland parts of Clarke Range near Eungella, Qld. Rainforest, small creeks.

BEHAVIOUR: White eggs laid in clump under rock in small pool or seepage area of creek at any time after rain. ♂ calls from on or under rock or vegetation near water.

CALL: Series of high-pitched 'tink, tink' notes.

KROOMBIT TOPS TINKER FROG
Taudactylus pleione

SIZE/ID: ♂ to 28mm, ♀ to 31mm. Grey, grey-brown to brown with darker markings. Dark stripe on side of head and body, bands across limbs. Skin granular. Fingers and toes with very small discs. Toes unwebbed.

HABITAT/RANGE: Critically endangered. Restricted to upland parts of Kroombit Tops, Qld. Rainforest streams.

BEHAVIOUR: Breeds in spring/summer after rain. Eggs and tadpoles unknown. ♂ calls from ground or up to 1.3m above stream.

CALL: Series of high-pitched metallic 'tink, tink' notes.

NORTHERN TINKER FROG
Taudactylus rheophilus

SIZE/ID: ♂ to 29mm, ♀ to 31mm. Brown with variable darker or lighter markings, often with broad dark band down back. Sides often dark, bands across limbs. Skin smooth to granular. Fingers and toes with very small discs. Toes unwebbed.

HABITAT/RANGE: Critically endangered. Restricted to upland forest on Mt Bellenden Ker range, Qld, if still existing. Rainforest streams.

BEHAVIOUR: Possibly breeds in spring/summer after rain. Tadpoles unknown. ♂ calls from among rocks or roots by stream.

CALL: Series of soft, rapid, metallic 'tink, tink' notes.

MONTANE TOADLET *Uperoleia altissima*

SIZE/ID: ♂ to 25mm, ♀ to 30mm. Grey or grey-brown with variable darker patches and spots. Parotoid glands small and yellowish, red patches in groin and behind knees, bands across legs. Skin with numerous tubercles. Toes unwebbed.

HABITAT/RANGE: Atherton and Windsor Ranges, north Qld. Forest and woodland near creeks.

BEHAVIOUR: Eggs laid singly in summer after rain, in creek pools. ♂ calls from ground.

CALL: Short, low-pitched, strident click.

DERBY TOADLET *Uperoleia aspera*

SIZE/ID: ♂ to 30mm, ♀ to 34mm. Brown with numerous evenly scattered dark spots. Parotoid glands moderate, beige or yellowish, red patches in groin and back of thighs, spots or bands on legs. Skin with numerous tubercles. Toes unwebbed.

HABITAT/RANGE: North-western Kimberley, WA. Woodland, grassland, floodplains near ephemeral ponds.

BEHAVIOUR: Eggs laid singly attached to vegetation in pools, after summer to autumn rain. ♂ calls from ground.

CALL: Short, loud click.

NORTHERN TOADLET *Uperoleia borealis*

SIZE/ID: ♂ and ♀ to 32mm. Brown with dark spots and patches. Parotoid glands prominent, beige or orange-brown, red patches in groin and back of thighs, bands on legs. Skin with numerous tubercles. Toes unwebbed.

HABITAT/RANGE: Far north-west NT to Kimberley region, WA. Low-lying woodland, flooded grassland and sandy spinifex, often near stony creeks or drainage lines.

BEHAVIOUR: Eggs laid singly attached to vegetation in pools, after summer to autumn rain. ♂ calls from base of tussock or crevice.

CALL: Short, low-pitched rasp with or without clicks.

FAT TOADLET *Uperoleia crassa*

SIZE/ID: ♂ to 30mm, ♀ to 31mm. Grey-brown with diffuse dark spots, darker by day. Parotoid glands prominent, beige or orange-brown, red patches in groin and back of thighs, bands on legs. Skin with numerous tubercles. Toes unwebbed.

HABITAT/RANGE: Far north-west Kimberley region, WA. Low-lying woodland, flooded grassland, sandy spinifex and rocky drainage lines.

BEHAVIOUR: Eggs laid singly after summer to autumn rain, attached to vegetation in pools. ♂ calls from base of tussock or crevice near water.

CALL: Short, low-pitched rasp.

HOWARD SPRINGS TOADLET *Uperoleia daviesae*

SIZE/ID: ♂ to 21mm, ♀ to 22mm. Grey or grey-brown with numerous brown-tipped raised tubercles, may have partial beige vertebral stripe and a few diffuse darker patches. Parotoid glands moderate, beige to red-brown, orange to red patches in groin and back of thighs, bands on legs. Toes unwebbed.

HABITAT/RANGE: Howard Springs to Elizabeth River catchments, NT. Low-lying sandy woodland swamps, flooded grassland and floodplain drainage areas.

BEHAVIOUR: Eggs laid singly attached to vegetation in pools, after summer rain. ♂ calls from base of tussock near water.

CALL: Short, resonant rasp.

DUSKY TOADLET *Uperoleia fusca*

SIZE/ID: ♂ to 28mm, ♀ to 29mm. Dark brown to grey with diffuse dark spots and patches, often with a paler crown. Parotoid glands moderate, tinged with brown. Yellow to orange-red patches in groin and back of thighs, patches on legs. Skin with numerous tubercles. Toes unwebbed.

HABITAT/RANGE: East coastal Australia from Eungella, Qld, to just south of Sydney, NSW. Ponds in forest, bushland or adjacent farmland.

BEHAVIOUR: Eggs laid singly after spring to autumn rain, attached to vegetation in pools. ♂ calls from base of tussock or leaf litter near water.

CALL: Short, low-pitched rasp.

GLANDULAR TOADLET *Uperoleia glandulosa*

SIZE/ID: ♂ to 30mm, ♀ to 28mm. Dark brown to grey-brown with diffuse or prominent dark spots and patches. Parotoid and other glands tipped with yellow-orange, orange-red patches in groin and back of thighs, patches on legs. Skin with numerous tubercles, sometimes forming partial yellow-brown vertebral line. Toes unwebbed.

HABITAT/RANGE: Northern Pilbara region, WA. River floodplains in dry woodland and ephemeral ponds in spinifex plains.

BEHAVIOUR: Eggs laid singly after summer rain, attached to vegetation in pools. ♂ calls from ground near water.

CALL: Single, sharp click.

FLOODPLAIN TOADLET *Uperoleia inundata*

SIZE/ID: ♂ to 28mm, ♀ to 32mm. Dark grey-brown to red-brown with diffuse darker patches in some. Parotoid glands prominent and red, brown or orange, red patches in groin and back of thighs. Skin with numerous tubercles, may be tipped with rusty red. Toes unwebbed.

HABITAT/RANGE: Northern Australia from north-west Qld to Kimberley, WA. Ephemeral ponds, floodplains and swamps, mostly in woodland.

BEHAVIOUR: Eggs laid singly after summer rain, attached aquatic vegetation. ♂ calls partly hidden at base of tussock or log.

CALL: Loud, resonant rasp.

SMOOTH TOADLET *Uperoleia laevigata*

SIZE/ID: ♂ to 28mm, ♀ to 32mm. Dark brown to light brown with dark spots and patches, may have paler crown. Parotoid glands prominent, lighter brown or beige, orange-red patches in groin and back of thighs, patches or bands on legs. Skin with numerous tubercles. Toes unwebbed.

HABITAT/RANGE: Eastern Australia from south-east Qld to north-east Vic. Ponds in drier forest, woodland or adjacent farmland.

BEHAVIOUR: Eggs laid singly after rain at any time, attached to aquatic vegetation. ♂ calls from leaf litter or grass, or while afloat.

CALL: Penetrating 'yerp' with upward inflection.

STONEMASON TOADLET *Uperoleia lithomoda*

SIZE/ID: ♂ to 26mm, ♀ to 30mm. Brown or grey-brown, often with darker patches. Parotoid and other glands prominent and pale yellow, orange-red patches in groin and back of thighs. Skin with numerous tubercles, some form partial cream or red vertebral line. Toes unwebbed.

HABITAT/RANGE: Northern Australia, north Qld to east Kimberley, WA. Ephemeral ponds in stony floodplains, grassland and swamps.

BEHAVIOUR: Eggs laid singly after summer to autumn rain, attached to aquatic vegetation. ♂ calls away from water or at base of tussock just in water.

CALL: Loud, explosive click.

LITTLEJOHN'S TOADLET *Uperoleia littlejohni*

SIZE/ID: ♂ to 31mm, ♀ to 29mm. Brown or grey-brown with darker patches. Parotoid and other glands prominent and pale salmon or beige, red patches in groin and back of thighs. Skin with numerous tubercles often tipped with salmon or beige. Toes unwebbed.

HABITAT/RANGE: Atherton Tableland to Burra Range, north Qld. Ephemeral creeks and ponds in dry stony woodland.

BEHAVIOUR: Eggs laid singly after summer rain, attached to aquatic vegetation. ♂ calls on ground among grass or leaf litter, often well back from water.

CALL: Short, low-pitched rasp.

MARTIN'S TOADLET *Uperoleia martini*

SIZE/ID: ♂ to 33mm, ♀ not known. Grey-brown to dark grey with darker patches, may have paler crown. Parotoid glands prominent, lighter rusty brown, yellow patches in groin, back of thighs and on arms. Skin with numerous tubercles. Toes unwebbed.

HABITAT/RANGE: Critically endangered. South-east NSW and Vic. Coastal heathland, ponds and swamps.

BEHAVIOUR: Eggs laid singly after summer to autumn rain, attached to aquatic vegetation. ♂ calls from grass in or near water.

CALL: Single pulsed note.

MJOBERG'S TOADLET *Uperoleia mjobergi*

SIZE/ID: ♂ and ♀ to 25mm. Brown with large, often symmetrical darker patches. Parotoid and other glands prominent and beige, red patches in groin and back of thighs, bands on legs. Skin with small tubercles. Toes unwebbed.

HABITAT/RANGE: North-west Kimberley, WA. Woodland, grassland, floodplains near ephemeral ponds.

BEHAVIOUR: Eggs laid singly after summer to autumn rain, attached to aquatic vegetation. ♂ calls from ground away from or near water.

CALL: Short, loud rasp.

WRINKLED TOADLET *Uperoleia rugosa*

SIZE/ID: ♂ to 32mm, ♀ to 30mm. Dark brown to light grey-brown with dark patches, often a V-shaped patch between eyes. Parotoid glands prominent, beige or yellow, orange-red patches in groin and back of thighs, bands on legs. Skin with numerous tubercles. Toes unwebbed.

HABITAT/RANGE: Eastern Qld and NSW, mostly west of ranges. Ponds in woodland or flooded grassland.

BEHAVIOUR: Eggs laid singly after spring to autumn rain, attached to aquatic vegetation. ♂ calls from leaf litter or grass, or in water.

CALL: Short, loud, low-pitched rasp.

RUSSELL'S TOADLET *Uperoleia russelli*

SIZE/ID: ♂ and ♀ to 33mm. Dark brown or grey-brown with small dark patches, often a V-shaped patch between eyes. Parotoid and other glands prominent, orange or brown, small red patch on back of thighs. Skin with numerous tubercles. Toes unwebbed.

HABITAT/RANGE: Carnarvon-Gascoyne river region, WA. Rivers or creeks.

BEHAVIOUR: Eggs laid singly after summer to autumn rain, attached to vegetation near edge of river or creek. ♂ calls from leaf litter or twigs on bank above water.

CALL: Fairly long rasp, sometimes with additional shorter rasps.

PILBARA TOADLET *Uperoleia saxatilis*

SIZE/ID: ♂ to 33mm, ♀ to 37mm. Brown or grey with small dark spots. Parotoid glands prominent, all glands orange-brown to red, minute red patch on back of thighs in some. Skin with numerous tubercles. Toes unwebbed.

HABITAT/RANGE: Pilbara region, WA. Ponds and flooded areas in spinifex plains and rocky creeks.

BEHAVIOUR: Eggs and tadpoles unknown. ♂ calls from rock, tussock or spinifex near water after heavy summer/autumn rain.

CALL: Low-pitched longer rasp, and shorter rasp.

MOLE TOADLET *Uperoleia talpa*

SIZE/ID: ♂ to 40mm, ♀ to 42mm. Our largest *Uperoleia*. Reddish-brown to dark brown with small darker spots. Parotoid and other glands very prominent, reddish-brown. Skin with numerous often red-tipped tubercles. Toes unwebbed.

HABITAT/RANGE: Kimberley to south-east Karratha, WA. Ponds and flooded areas in woodland, grassland and river catchments.

BEHAVIOUR: Eggs laid singly, attached to vegetation after summer to autumn rain. ♂ calls among leaf litter, near tussocks or rocks.

CALL: Loud, fairly high-pitched 'yerp' followed by similar but longer note.

TYLER'S TOADLET *Uperoleia tyleri*

SIZE/ID: ♂ to 33mm, ♀ to 34mm. Dark brown to very dark grey with darker spots and patches, may have paler crown. Parotoid glands very prominent, yellow-brown to reddish-brown, yellow patches in groin, back of thighs and on arms. Skin with numerous tubercles. Toes unwebbed.

HABITAT/RANGE: South-east NSW. Coastal heathland, permanent ponds and swamps.

BEHAVIOUR: Eggs laid singly, attached to vegetation in pools after summer to autumn rain. ♂ calls from grass in or near water.

CALL: Short, low-pitched rasp.

NORTHERN TERRITORY FROG
Austrochaperina adelphe

SIZE/ID: ♂ to 19mm, ♀ to 22mm. Brown or grey-brown, some with darker flecks, dark stripe on side of head to arm, sides of body may be mottled. Skin smooth. Fingers and toes unwebbed with narrow discs.

HABITAT/RANGE: Northern NT. Monsoon forest, *Melaleuca* swamps and sandstone plateaus.

BEHAVIOUR: Large white eggs laid singly in hidden nest beneath moist leaf litter, after summer rain. No tadpole stage, embryos develop to froglets in egg capsules, attended by ♂. ♂ calls hidden on ground.

CALL: Series of rapid high-pitched peeps.

FRY'S FROG *Austrochaperina fryi*

SIZE/ID: ♂ to 30mm, ♀ to 35mm. Brown, red or yellow, variable darker flecks or cream vertebral stripe. Dark stripe on side of head to arm. Skin smooth. Fingers and toes unwebbed with rounded discs.

HABITAT/RANGE: Northern Wet Tropics, Qld, Lamb Range to south Cooktown. Rainforest from near sea-level to 1,340m.

BEHAVIOUR: Large white eggs laid singly in nest on ground beneath moist leaf litter, after summer rain. No tadpole stage, embryos develop to froglets in egg capsules, attended by ♂. ♂ calls hidden on ground.

CALL: Series of short high-pitched whistle-like notes.

RAIN WHISTLING FROG *Austrochaperina pluvialis*

SIZE/ID: ♂ to 26mm, ♀ to 29mm. Brown, grey or golden with darker or lighter mottling, silver-white or cream stripe on side of head to body, dark brown beneath this. Skin smooth. Fingers and toes unwebbed with small discs.

HABITAT/RANGE: Wet Tropics, Qld. Rainforest above 20m.

BEHAVIOUR: Large white eggs laid singly in nest on ground beneath rocks or moist leaf litter, after summer rain. No tadpole stage, embryos develop to froglets in egg capsules, attended by ♂. ♂ calls hidden on ground.

CALL: Short series of high-pitched whistle-like notes.

ROBUST WHISTLING FROG
Austrochaperina robusta

SIZE/ID: ♂ to 26mm, ♀ to 29mm. Brown, grey or golden with darker or lighter mottling, pale stripe on side of head to body with dark brown beneath. Skin smooth. Fingers and toes unwebbed with small discs.

HABITAT/RANGE: Southern Wet Tropics, Qld, Bluewater Range to Lamb Range. Rainforest above 350m.

BEHAVIOUR: Large white eggs laid singly in nest on ground beneath rocks or moist leaf litter, after summer rain. No tadpole stage, embryos develop to froglets in egg capsules, attended by ♂. ♂ calls hidden on ground.

CALL: Short series of high-pitched chirrups.

TAPPING NURSERY FROG *Cophixalus aenigma*

SIZE/ID: ♂ and ♀ to 23mm. Brown, grey or orange to almost black, variable dark flecks or broad vertebral stripe. Pale crown in some. Skin smooth. Fingers and toes unwebbed with discs.

HABITAT/RANGE: Wet Tropics, Qld, populations in a few ranges. Rainforest and boulder fields above 700m.

BEHAVIOUR: Large white eggs laid in connected string in nest beneath rocks or rotting logs after summer rain. No tadpole stage, embryos develop to froglets in egg capsules, attended by ♂. ♂ calls from ground or partly elevated.

CALL: Series of fast tapping sounds.

BUZZING NURSERY FROG *Cophixalus bombiens*

SIZE/ID: ♂ to 14mm, ♀ to 17mm. Brown, grey, beige or red, variable darker flecks or patches. Dark line on side of head, pale crown in some. Skin with some tubercles and folds. Fingers and toes unwebbed with small discs.

HABITAT/RANGE: Northern Wet Tropics, Qld. Rainforest from lowland areas to lower slopes of some ranges.

BEHAVIOUR: Large white eggs in connected string in nest beneath logs, after summer rain. No tadpole stage, embryos develop to froglets in egg capsules, attended by ♂. ♂ calls hidden on ground.

CALL: Short, high-pitched buzzing.

RATTLING NURSERY FROG *Cophixalus crepitans*

SIZE/ID: ♂ and ♀ to 14mm. Brown or grey with darker or paler patches, distinct in some. Dark line on side of head, most have pale crown. Skin with some tubercles. Fingers and toes unwebbed with distinct discs.

HABITAT/RANGE: Near threatened. McIlwraith Range, Cape York, Qld. Rainforest and monsoon vine forest.

BEHAVIOUR: Breeding unknown but likely to be similar to other members of *Cophixalus*, with no tadpole stage and embryos developing to froglets in egg capsules. ♂ calls from elevated site.

CALL: Short, rattling sound with two clicks.

HOSMER'S NURSERY FROG *Cophixalus hosmeri*

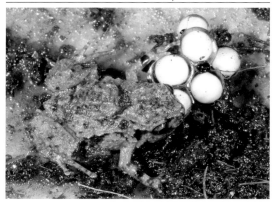

SIZE/ID: ♂ to 14mm, ♀ to at least 17mm. Brown or grey, with darker patches and pinkish areas in some. Dark or cream streak on side of head. Skin smooth or with tubercles and ridges. Fingers and toes unwebbed with distinct discs.

HABITAT/RANGE: Carbine Tableland, Wet Tropics, Qld. Montane rainforest above 960m.

BEHAVIOUR: Large white eggs laid in connected string in palm axils, no tadpole stage, embryos develop to froglets in egg capsules, attended by ♂. ♂ calls while elevated in palm axil.

CALL: Medium to fast tapping or buzzing sound.

KUTINI BOULDER FROG *Cophixalus kulakula*

SIZE/ID: ♂ to 45mm, ♀ to 48mm. Brown or grey with faint darker patches in some. Dark stripe on side of head, paler crown. Skin with numerous tubercles. Fingers and toes long and unwebbed with large discs.

HABITAT/RANGE: Mt Tozer, Cape York Peninsula, Qld. Granite boulder fields and rocks in rainforest gullies.

BEHAVIOUR: Breeding unknown, but large white eggs likely to be laid in similar manner to other members of *Cophixalus*. ♂ leads ♀ to nest site in rocks while calling.

CALL: Short, wavering bleat.

GOLDEN-CAPPED BOULDER FROG
Cophixalus pakayakulangan

SIZE/ID: ♂ to 47mm, ♀ to 53mm. Our largest microhylid. Brown or grey with diffuse darker patches or mottling in some. Dark stripe on sides of head, yellow crown in ♂. Skin with small tubercles. Fingers and toes long and unwebbed with large discs.

HABITAT/RANGE: South of Stanly Hill, Cape York Peninsula, Qld. Granite boulder piles in vine forest.

BEHAVIOUR: Breeding unknown, but large white eggs likely to be laid in similar manner to other members of *Cophixalus*.

CALL: Unknown.

NORTHERN ORNATE NURSERY FROG
Cophixalus ornatus

SIZE/ID: ♂ and ♀ to 29mm. Brown, grey or cream, patches of black, brown, orange, red or yellow and a broad vertebral band in some. Dark line on side of head. Skin smooth or with tubercles and ridges. Fingers and toes unwebbed with broad discs.

HABITAT/RANGE: Northern Wet Tropics, Qld. Rainforest above 330m.

BEHAVIOUR: Large white eggs laid in connected string. ♂ leads ♀ to ground nest while calling. No tadpole stage, embryos develop directly to frogs in capsules. ♂ calls while elevated.

CALL: High-pitched, strident 'beep'.

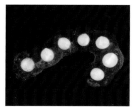

Stage 1, large round eggs in string

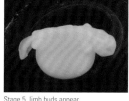

Stage 5, limb buds appear

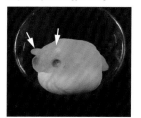

Stage 6, eyes visible, circulation begins

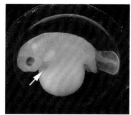

Stage 7, longer limbs and tail

Stage 8, head broader, first gut loop

Stage 15, froglet about to hatch

BLACK MOUNTAIN BOULDER FROG
Cophixalus saxatilis

SIZE/ID: ♂ to 35mm, ♀ to 47mm. Olive-brown or yellow with darker mottling in ♂, ♀ yellow-brown. Skin with small tubercles. Fingers and toes long and unwebbed with broad discs.

HABITAT/RANGE: Black Mountain (Trevathan Range), north Qld. Among massive piles of granite boulders forming hills.

BEHAVIOUR: Large white eggs laid in connected string in rock crevice up to 25m beneath surface of rock piles. ♂ leads ♀ to nest site while calling. No tadpole stage, large white eggs develop to froglets in egg capsules, attended by ♂.

CALL: Slow, low-pitched tapping.

CAPE MELVILLE BOULDER FROG
Cophixalus zweifeli

SIZE/ID: ♂ and ♀ to 45mm. ♀ brown with a few black blotches on sides and red in groin and backs of legs. ♂ has golden crown and diffuse mottling. Skin mostly smooth. Fingers and toes long and unwebbed with broad discs.

HABITAT/RANGE: Cape Melville National Park, north Qld. Among massive piles of granite boulders forming hills.

BEHAVIOUR: Breeding unknown, likely to be similar to *C. saxatilis*.

CALL: Unknown.

WATER FROG *Hylarana daemeli*

SIZE/ID: ♂ to 58mm, ♀ to 81mm. Long pointed snout. Brown, olive-brown or bronze with long dorsolateral skin fold on each side from behind eye to lower back. Lemon over sides and in groin, bands across legs. Skin smooth or with small tubercles. Fingers and toes with small discs, toes fully webbed.

HABITAT/RANGE: North Qld from north of Townsville to tip of Cape York Peninsula. Creeks, swamps and permanent ponds in forest.

BEHAVIOUR: Eggs laid in floating film in pools. Tadpoles develop in water. ♂ calls on ground or rock near water.

CALL: Soft quavering bleat.

CANE TOAD *Rhinella marina*

SIZE/ID: ♂ to 100mm, ♀ to 150mm. Brown, some with darker blotches, belly-sides mottled. Thick ridges on eyelids and snout, very large, toxic parotoid glands on shoulders. Skin dry and leathery with tubercles. Fingers and toes unwebbed.

HABITAT/RANGE: Introduced to north Qld in 1935, spread to mid-coastal NSW and across northern Australia through Kimberley region. Any habitat. Toxic from eggs to adults to most native fauna.

BEHAVIOUR: Feeds on anything that moves, but also pet food. Lays up to 35,000 eggs in long chains in ponds and creek pools.

CALL: Hollow, low-pitched rolling trill like telephone dial-tone.

INDEX

INDEX

OTHER TITLES IN THE REED CONCISE GUIDES SERIES

Animals of Australia (ISBN 978 1 92151 754 9)

Wildflowers of Australia (ISBN 978 1 92151 755 6)

Birds of Australia (ISBN 978 1 92151 753 2)